FREEDOM OR TOLERANCE?

FREEDOM OR TOLERANCE?

The Declaration on Religious Freedom of Vatican Council II

THE TEXT WITH COMMENTARY
IN THE CONTEXT OF THE
CHURCH-STATE DISCUSSION

by

ENDA MCDONAGH

Professor of Moral Theology
St Patrick's College, Maynooth, Ireland

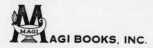

MAGI BOOKS, INC.

NIHIL OBSTAT John M. T. Barton S.T.D., L.S.S., *Censor*
IMPRIMATUR ✠ Patrick Casey Vic. Gen., Westminster, 3rd
   February 1967.
   The Nihil obstat *and* Imprimatur *are a declaration that a book or
pamphlet is considered to be free from doctrinal or moral error. It is not
implied that those who have granted the* Nihil obstat *and* Imprimatur
agree with the contents, opinions or statements expressed.

© 1967 Enda McDonagh
First published in the United States in 1967
by Magi Books Inc.
33 Buckingham Drive, Albany, New York 12208
Printed in Great Britain by Billing & Sons Ltd.
Guildford and London

Contents

Note and Acknowledgements

In the essays written before the Declaration, 'public order' does not include what is generally called public morality. In the Declaration (§7) public order is used to cover public morality as well. V. supra pp. 67–69.

The author is indebted to the Furrow Trust and to the Irish Theological Quarterly for permission to use matter already published by them.

1. Introduction

The *Declaration on Religious Freedom* issued by the
Second Vatican Council marked a decisive stage in
the development of Roman Catholic thinking on this
topic. For some people within and without the Roman
Church it seemed not merely a stage in development
but a complete reversal of the Church's previous position. The 'glorious minority' as one of their supporters
called them, who fought the Declaration by every
Conciliar and some extra-Conciliar means, were
clearly convinced that the proposed Declaration
could not be regarded as merely a development of the
hitherto accepted teaching. And in this they would
have the agreement of some of the most ardent supporters of the Declaration, Roman and non-Roman.
In its progress and final realisation as a conciliar
document the *Declaration on Religious Freedom* will
present a fascinating case-history for the future
historian of Vatican II. Its role in the understanding
of doctrinal development within the Church may,
however, prove to be of more lasting significance.
Anyone who has followed even vaguely the debates of
the last fifteen years on religious freedom must have
had some sense of the community's struggle to do
justice to all the elements in its own tradition in seeking an answer to the contemporary question on religious freedom. But it is when one surveys not fifteen

years but nineteen hundred years of Church history
that one is made aware of the complex movements
which were ultimately brought together in one
apparently simple document at Vatican II.

Christ's message, it was clear from the beginning,
could only be accepted in freedom. It did not need
and could not use the instruments of domination
proper to this world. For His kingdom was not of this
world. Yet it recognised the kingdoms of this world,
the obligation to render Caesar his own, to obey
political rulers and to do it for conscience' sake. The
new kingdom was not in competition with political
kingdoms. The kingdom of Israel was not to be
restored as a political entity. Yet Christians by their
own claims, formed a distinct and exclusive if
exclusively religious society. This was hard for their
first contemporaries, especially contemporaries with
political power, the Roman Emperors, their consuls
and proconsuls, to grasp. The early energies of the
Christians had to be directed into defending their
freedom as individuals and communities, denying any
political ambitions and sharply distinguishing the
religious from the political community – for example
the Apologists writing in the second century and more
forcibly and effectively Tertullian at the beginning
of the third. Right up to the time of the Edict of
Milan freedom of religion and its historically inseparable counterpart the distinction between the political
and the religious were clearly maintained by Christian
writers.

During that long, complex development in the
relations between the political and the religious
powers, after the first recognition of freedom for
Christianity and then its authorisation as an official
religion, the religious freedom of the individual and
the distinction between the political and religious
spheres underwent periods of obscurity, and indeed

eclipse. The story down to and including the Reformation is told in detail and with remarkable sensitivity by Joseph Lecler in his two-volume work *Histoire de la Tolérance au Siècle de la Reforme.*[1]

An attempt to summarise such a complicated story would be foolish. But some of the theological and practical issues which were important may be worth mentioning. In general, one could maintain that the two basic principles, the individual's freedom to accept or reject the faith and the distinction of religion and politics, persisted in the Church's teaching. They were naturally more strongly insisted upon against a civil authority hostile to the Church, or to a particular Church authority, pope or bishop. A typical instance of this was the reign of Constantius, son of Constantine (350–361) at the time of the Arian heresy. But it has recurred constantly. And in the framework of relations between political and religious authorities which we have known, such insistence on freedom and distinction, or lack of insistence, depended almost inevitably on the diplomatic top-level relationships between Rome and civil ruler. This has happened in the very recent past and with some tragic consequences.

In medieval times, however, the political-religious distinction became obscured in the notion of Christendom with its two powers, religious and political, governing really only one society. So the religious defector, the heretic, was regarded as a civil outlaw. Adding this to the fact that it seemed impossible to the medievals to conceive of somebody leaving the true Church in good faith, medieval churchmen saw nothing wrong with invoking the 'civil arm' to deal with heretics. Alternatively, non-Christians and Jews were given a protection and citizenship, however limited, not accorded to 'heretics', and the freedom of

[1] Translated as *Tolerance and Reformation*, Longmans, 1960.

first acceptance of the faith was strongly insisted upon. Similarly the distinction between politics and religion survived in however attenuated a form.

The Reformation period with the elevation of the prince to be religious head of the Church in some reformed churches in theory and the adopting of the practical consequences of this by many Catholic princes, issued in the religious wars, strictly religious persecution and dissolution of the religion-politics distinction in the principle *cuius regio eius religio.*

Religious restrictions by the princes were generally more a matter of political expediency than of religious zeal. And political expediency in turn later demanded and ensured a certain religious freedom. Indeed, as Father Lecler points out, at the beginning of the seventeenth century with the exception of Brandenburg, the only states practising legal tolerance for dissident sects were the Catholic states of France, Poland, Austria and Bohemia. And it is worth recalling here that in North America, haven of refugees from religious persecution, Maryland, under its first Catholic founders, provided for religious freedom for all until Catholics lost power and freedom.

However this legal tolerance based on political needs had a chequered history and did not issue in any doctrine or any inviolable right of religious freedom. Other forces were at work. The growth of religious indifference, partly in reaction to the religious wars and intolerance but based more on certain intellectual movements prepared the way for a more doctrinaire idea of the freedom of religion. As it was joined with the revolutionary forces at the beginning of the nineteenth century who associated the Church and religion very closely with the *Ancien Régime* which they wished to overthrow, this doctrine of religious freedom emerged in Europe from sources hostile to the Church. In theory and in practice it proved unacceptable to the Church. In theory it was based on the principle of religious indifference. One religion is as good or as bad, as true or as false as another. At any rate it is of no particular importance. Further its theory of the omnicompetent state demolished at once the distinction between politics and religion and any genuine religious freedom. Politics was all and the existence of religious groups depended on the will of the supreme all-embracing state-authority.

It is against this background that the papal statements of the nineteenth century of Gregory XVI, Pius IX and Leo XIII, condemning religious freedom as then proclaimed, must be judged. And in the calmer days of Leo XIII the outline of an acceptable approach to religious freedom may again be discerned in his return to the basic distinction between politics and religion, between the state and Church, their supremacy and independence in their respective spheres, his insistence on the freedom of the Church as the first and overriding principle in Church-State relations and his approval in practice of legal toleration in particular states for the good of the community.

This acceptance in practice of legal tolerance, as shown for example in the approval of the Belgian Constitution of 1830, had never been abandoned despite the strong condemnatory nature of the statements of Gregory XVI and Pius IX on the theory. In their historical context the papal teaching and practice is understandable, although it may be regretted that the insights of people like Lacordaire, Montalembert and Lamennais were not further explored or that the very different situation and attitudes in North America and Ireland for instance were not allowed to influence papal teaching policy.

The twentieth century saw a great development in the social organisation of the state, the emergence of a

quite different threat to Christian existence in the
various totalitarian régimes and cast the Church in
the role of defender of the rights of the individual.
The defence by Pius XI and Pius XII of the rights of
the individual led to some development in the notion
of religious freedom also. It was, however, with
Pacem in Terris of John XXIII and the Council's
Declaration that the Church's position was affirmed
clearly beyond yea or nay as upholding religious freedom.

In the final years of development the work of
individuals like John Courtney Murray in the United
States as well as a number of European scholars were
decisive. Their insistence on the historical nature of
previous Church-State relationships and of papal
documents on the matter proved to be the solution to
many difficulties.

It was in the later years of this controversy from
1960–63 that essays in the second half of this book
were written. They grew out of a doctorate study
presented at Munich University on *Church and State
in the Constitution of Ireland*. As a result of that work I
was convinced that a clear statement on the lines of
the Declaration was necessary and these essays were
an attempt to support the work of Fr Murray and
others by writing within the context of a state that
was ninety-five per cent Catholic and yet in its
Constitution guaranteed complete religious freedom.

These chapters 5–8, then, provide some evidence
of the pre-Conciliar debate. They also serve to spell
out in particular detail some of the background and
implications of the doctrine of religious freedom which
was promulgated by Vatican II.

2. The Declaration of Vatican II on Religious Freedom

*on the right of
the person and of
communities to social
and civil freedom in
matters religious*

1. A sense of the dignity of the human person has been impressing itself more and more deeply on the consciousness of contemporary man.[1] And the demand is increasingly made that men should act on their own judgement, enjoying and making use of a responsible freedom, not driven by coercion but motivated by a sense of duty. The demand is also made that constitutional limits should be set to the powers of government, in order that there may be no encroachment on the rightful freedom of the person and of associations.

This demand for freedom in human society chiefly regards the quest for the values proper to the human spirit. It regards, in the first place, the free exercise of religion in society.

[1] Cf. John XXIII, encyclical *Pacem in Terris*, 11 April 1963: AAS 55 (1963), p. 279; ibid., p. 265; Pius XII, radio message, 24 December 1944; AAS 37 (1945), p. 14.

This Vatican Synod takes careful note of these
desires in the minds of men. It proposes to declare
them to be greatly in accord with truth and justice.
To this end, it searches into the sacred tradition
and doctrine of the Church – the treasury out of
which the Church continually brings forth new
things that are in harmony with the things that are
old.

First, this sacred Synod professes its belief that
God himself has made known to mankind the way
in which men are to serve Him, and thus be saved
in Christ and come to blessedness. We believe that
this one true religion subsists in the catholic and
apostolic Church, to which the Lord Jesus committed the duty of spreading it abroad among all
men. Thus He spoke to the apostles: 'Go, therefore, and make disciples of all nations, baptising
them in the name of the Father, and of the Son,
and of the Holy Spirit, teaching them to observe
all that I have commanded you' (Matt. 28:19–20).
On their part, all men are bound to seek the truth,
especially in what concerns God and His Church,
and to embrace the truth they come to know, and
to hold fast to it.

This sacred Synod likewise professes its belief
that it is upon the human conscience that these
obligations fall and exert their binding force. The
truth cannot impose itself except by virtue of its
own truth, as it makes its entrance into the mind
at once quietly and with power. Religious freedom,
in turn, which men demand as necessary to fulfil
their duty to worship God, has to do with immunity
from coercion in civil society. Therefore, it leaves
untouched traditional Catholic doctrine on the
moral duty of men and societies toward the true
religion and toward the one Church of Christ.

Over and above all this, in taking up the matter

of religious freedom this sacred Synod intends to develop the doctrine of recent Popes on the inviolable rights of the human person and on the constitutional order of society.

General Principle on Religious Freedom

2. This Vatican Synod declares that the human person has a right to religious freedom. This freedom means that all men are to be immune from coercion on the part of individuals or of social groups and of any human power, in such wise that in matters religious no one is to be forced to act in a manner contrary to his own beliefs. Nor is anyone to be restrained from acting in accordance with his own beliefs, whether privately or publicly, whether alone or in association with others, within due limits.

The Synod further declares that the right to religious freedom has its foundation in the very dignity of the human person, as this dignity is known through the revealed Word of God and by reason itself.[2] This right of the human person to religious freedom is to be recognised in the constitutional law whereby society is governed. Thus it is to become a civil right.

It is in accordance with their dignity as persons – that is, beings endowed with reason and free will and therefore privileged to bear personal responsibility – that all men should be at once impelled by nature and also bound by a moral obligation to seek the truth, especially religious truth. They are

[2] Cf. John XXIII, encyclical *Pacem in Terris*, 11 April 1963: AAS 55 (1963), pp. 260–261; Pius XII, radio message, 24 December 1942: AAS 35 (1943), p. 19; Pius XI, encyclical *Mit Brennender Sorge*, 14 March 1937: AAS 29 (1937), p. 160; Leo XIII, encyclical *Libertas Praestantissimum*, 20 June 1888: Acts of Leo XIII 8 (1888), pp. 237–238.

also bound to adhere to the truth, once it is known, and to order their whole lives in accord with the demands of truth.

However, men cannot discharge these obligations in a manner in keeping with their own nature unless they enjoy immunity from external coercion as well as psychological freedom. Therefore, the right to religious freedom has its foundation, not in the subjective disposition of the person, but in his very nature. In consequence, the right to this immunity continues to exist even in those who do not live up to their obligation of seeking the truth and adhering to it. Nor is the exercise of this right to be impeded, provided that the just requirements of public order are observed.

3. Further light is shed on the subject if one considers that the highest norm of human life is the divine law – eternal, objective, and universal – whereby God orders, directs, and governs the entire universe and all the ways of the human community, by a plan conceived in wisdom and love. Man has been made by God to participate in this law, with the result that, under the gentle disposition of divine Providence, he can come to perceive ever increasingly the unchanging truth. Hence every man has the duty, and therefore the right, to seek the truth in matters religious, in order that he may with prudence form for himself right and true judgements of conscience, with the use of all suitable means.

Truth, however, is to be sought after in a manner proper to the dignity of the human person and his social nature. The inquiry is to be free, carried on with the aid of teaching or instruction, communication, and dialogue. In the course of these, men explain to one another the truth they have discovered, or think they have discovered, in order thus to assist one another in the quest for truth. Moreover, as the truth is discovered, it is by a personal assent that men are to adhere to it.

On his part, man perceives and acknowledges the imperatives of the divine law through the mediation of conscience. In all his activity a man is bound to follow his conscience faithfully, in order that he may come to God, for whom he was created. It follows that he is not to be forced to act in a manner contrary to his conscience. Nor, on the other hand, is he to be restrained from acting in accordance with his conscience, especially in matters religious.

For, of its very nature, the exercise of religion consists before all else in those internal, voluntary, and free acts whereby man sets the course of his life directly toward God. No merely human power can either command or prohibit acts of this kind.[3]

However, the social nature of man itself requires that he should give external expression to his internal acts of religion; that he should participate with others in matters religious; that he should profess his religion in community. Injury, therefore, is done to the human person and to the very order established by God for human life, if the free exercise of religion is denied in society when the just requirements of public order do not so require.

There is a further consideration. The religious acts whereby men, in private and in public and out of a sense of personal conviction, direct their lives to God transcend by their very nature the order of terrestrial and temporal affairs. Government, therefore, ought ought indeed to take account of

[3] Cf. John XXIII, encyclical *Pacem in Terris*, 11 April 1963: AAS 55 (1963), p. 270; Paul VI, radio message, 22 December 1964: AAS 57 (1965), pp. 181–182.

the religious life of the people and show it favour since the function of government is to make provision for the common welfare. However, it would clearly transgress the limits set to its power were it to presume to direct or inhibit acts that are religious.

4. The freedom or immunity from coercion in matters religious which is the endowment of persons as individuals is also to be recognised as their right when they act in community. Religious bodies are a requirement of the social nature both of man and of religion itself.

Provided the just requirements of public order are observed, religious bodies rightfully claim freedom in order that they may govern themselves according to their own norms, honour the Supreme Being in public worship, assist their members in the practice of the religious life, strengthen them by instruction, and promote institutions in which they may join together for the purpose of ordering their own lives in accordance with their religious principles.

Religious bodies also have the right not to be hindered, either by legal measures or by administrative action on the part of government, in the selection, training, appointment, and transferral of their own ministers, in communicating with religious authorities and communities abroad, in erecting buildings for religious purposes, and in the acquisition and use of suitable funds or properties.

Religious bodies also have the right not to be hindered in their public teaching and witness to their faith, whether by the spoken or by the written word. However, in spreading religious faith and in introducing religious practices, everyone ought at all times to refrain from any manner of action which might seem to carry a hint of coercion or of a kind of persuasion that would be dishonourable or unworthy, especially when dealing with poor or uneducated people. Such a manner of action would have to be considered an abuse of one's own right and a violation of the right of others.

In addition, it comes within the meaning of religious freedom that religious bodies should not be prohibited from freely undertaking to show the special value of their doctrine in what concerns the organization of society and the inspiration of the whole of human activity. Finally, the social nature of man and the very nature of religion afford the foundation of the right of men freely to hold meetings and to establish educational, cultural, charitable, and social organisations, under the impulse of their own religious sense.

5. Since the family is a society in its own original right, it has the right freely to live its own domestic religious life under the guidance of parents. Parents, moreover, have the right to determine, in accordance with their own religious beliefs, the kind of religious education that their children are to receive.

Government, in consequence, must acknowledge the right of parents to make a genuinely free choice of schools and of other means of education. The use of this freedom of choice is not to be made a reason for imposing unjust burdens on parents, whether directly or indirectly. Besides, the rights of parents are violated if their children are forced to attend lessons or instruction which are not in agreement with their religious beliefs. The same is true if a single system of education, from which all religious formation is excluded, is imposed upon all.

6. The common welfare of society consists in the

entirety of those conditions of social life under which men enjoy the possibility of achieving their own perfection in a certain fullness of measure and also with some relative ease. Hence this welfare consists chiefly in the protection of the rights,[4] and in the performance of the duties, of the human person. Therefore, the care of the right to religious freedom devolves upon the people as a whole, upon social groups, upon government, and upon the Church and other religious Communities, in virtue of the duty of all toward the common welfare, and in the manner proper to each.

The protection and promotion of the inviolable rights of man ranks among the essential duties of government.[5] Therefore, government is to assume the safeguard of the religious freedom of all its citizens, in an effective manner, by just laws and by other appropriate means. Government is also to help create conditions favourable to the fostering of religious life, in order that the people may be truly enabled to exercise their religious rights and to fulfil their religious duties, and also in order that society itself may profit by the moral qualities of justice and peace which have their origin in men's faithfulness to God and to His holy will.[6]

If, in view of peculiar circumstances obtaining among certain peoples, special legal recognition is given in the constitutional order of society to one religious body, it is at the same time imperative that the right of all citizens and religious bodies to

[4] Cf. John XXIII, encyclical *Mater et Magistra*, 15 May 1961: AAS 53 (1961), p. 417; idem, encyclical *Pacem in Terris*, 11 April 1963: AAS 55 (1963), p. 273.

[5] Cf. John XXIII, encyclical *Pacem in Terris*, 11 April 1963: AAS 55 (1963), pp. 273–274; Pius XII, radio message, 1 June 1941: AAS 33 (1941), p. 200.

[6] Cf. Leo XIII, encyclical *Immortale Dei*, 1 November 1885: AAS 18 (1885), p. 161.

religious freedom should be recognised and made effective in practice.

Finally, government is to see to it that the equality of citizens before the law, which is itself an element of the common welfare, is never violated for religious reasons, whether openly or covertly. Nor is there to be discrimination among citizens.

It follows that a wrong is done when government imposes upon its people, by force or fear or other means, the profession or repudiation of any religion, or when it hinders men from joining or leaving a religious body. All the more is it a violation of the will of God and of the sacred rights of the person and the family of nations, when force is brought to bear in any way in order to destroy or repress religion, either in the whole of mankind or in a particular country or in a specific community.

7. The right to religious freedom is exercised in human society; hence its exercise is subject to certain regulatory norms. In the use of all freedoms, the moral principle of personal and social responsibility is to be observed. In the exercise of their rights, individual men and social groups are bound by the moral law to have respect both for the rights of others and for their own duties toward others and for the common welfare of all. Men are to deal with their fellows in justice and civility.

Furthermore, society has the right to defend itself against possible abuses committed on pretext of freedom of religion. It is the special duty of government to provide this protection. However, government is not to act in arbitrary fashion or in an unfair spirit of partisanship. Its action is to be controlled by juridical norms which are in conformity with the objective moral order.

These norms arise out of the need for effective

safeguard of the rights of all citizens and for peaceful settlement of conflicts of rights. They flow from the need for an adequate care of genuine public peace, which comes about when men live together in good order and in true justice. They come, finally, out of the need for a proper guardianship of public morality. These matters constitute the basic component of the common welfare: they are what is meant by public order.

For the rest, the usages of society are to be the usages of freedom in their full range. These require that the freedom of man be respected as far as possible, and curtailed only when and in so far as necessary.

8. Many pressures are brought to bear upon men of our day, to the point where the danger arises lest they lose the possibility of acting on their own judgement. On the other hand, not a few can be found who seem inclined to use the name of freedom as the pretext for refusing to submit to authority and for making light of the duty of obedience.

Therefore, this Vatican Synod urges everyone, especially those who are charged with the task of educating others, to do their utmost to form men who will respect the moral order and be obedient to lawful authority. Let them form men too who will be lovers of true freedom – men, in other words, who will come to decisions on their own judgement and in the light of truth, govern their activities with a sense of responsibility, and strive after what is true and right, willing always to join with others in co-operative effort.

Religious freedom, therefore, ought to have this further purpose and aim, namely, that men may come to act with greater responsibility in fulfilling their duties in community life.

Religious Freedom in the Light of Revelation

9. The declaration of this Vatican Synod on the right of man to religious freedom has its foundation in the dignity of the person. The requirements of this dignity have come to be more adequately known to human reason through centuries of experience. What is more, this doctrine of freedom has roots in divine revelation, and for this reason Christians are bound to respect it all the more conscientiously.

Revelation does not indeed affirm in so many words the right of man to immunity from external coercion in matters religious. It does, however, disclose the dignity of the human person in its full dimensions. It gives evidence of the respect which Christ showed toward the freedom with which man is to fulfil his duty of belief in the Word of God. It gives us lessons too in the spirit which disciples of such a Master ought to make their own and to follow in every situation.

Thus, further light is cast on the general principles upon which the doctrine of this Declaration on Religious Freedom is based. In particular, religious freedom in society is entirely consonant with the freedom of the act of Christian faith.

10. It is one of the major tenets of Catholic doctrine that man's response to God in faith must be free. Therefore no one is to be forced to embrace the Christian faith[7] against his own will. This doctrine is contained in the Word of God and it was con-

---

[7] Cf. CIC, c. 1351; Pius XII, allocution to prelate auditors and other officials and administrators of the tribune of the Holy Roman Rota, 6 October 1946: AAS 38 (1946), p. 394; idem, encyclical *Mystici Corporis*, 29 June 1943: AAS (1943), p. 243.

stantly proclaimed by the Fathers of the Church.[8]
The act of faith is of its very nature a free act. Man,
redeemed by Christ the Saviour and through
Christ Jesus called to be God's adopted son,[9] cannot give his adherence to God revealing Himself
unless the Father draw him[10] to offer to God the
reasonable and free submission of faith.

It is therefore completely in accord with the
nature of faith that in matters religious every
manner of coercion on the part of men should be
excluded. In consequence, the principle of religious
freedom makes no small contribution to the creation
of an environment in which men can without
hindrance be invited to Christian faith, and embrace it of their own free will, and profess it effectively in their whole manner of life.

11. God calls men to serve Him in spirit and in
truth. Hence they are bound in conscience but
they stand under no compulsion. God has regard
for the dignity of the human person whom He
Himself created; man is to be guided by his own
judgement and he is to enjoy freedom.

[8] Cf. Lactantius *Divinarum Institutionum*, Book V, 19: CSEL
19, pp. 463–464, 465: PL 6, 614 and 616 (ch. 20); St Ambrose,
Epistola ad Valentianum Imp., Letter 21: PL 16, 1005; St Augus-
tine, *Contra Litteras Petiliani*, Book II, ch. 83: CSEL 52, p. 112:
PL 43, 315; cf. C. 23, q. 5, c. 33 (ed. Friedberg, col. 939); idem,
Letter 23: PL 33, 98; idem, Letter 34: PL 33, 132; idem, Letter
35: PL 33, 135; St Gregory the Great, *Epistola ad Virgilium et
Theodorum Episcopos Massiliae Galliarum*, Register of Letters I,
45: MGH Ep. 1, p. 72; PL 77, 510–511 (Book I, ep. 47); idem,
Epistola ad Johannem Episcopum Constantinopolitanum, Register of
Letters, III, 52: MGH Letter 1, p. 210: PL 77, 649 (Book III,
Letter 53); cf. D. 45, c. 1 (ed. Friedberg, col. 160); Council of
Toledo IV, c. 57: Mansi 10, 633; cf. D. 45, c. 5 (ed. Friedberg,
col. 161–162); Clement III: X., V. 6, 9: ed. Friedberg, col. 774;
Innocent III, *Epistola ad Arelatensem Archiepiscopum*, X., III, 42, 3:
ed. Friedberg, col. 646.
[9] Cf. Eph. 1:5.   [10] Cf. Jn. 6:44.

This truth appears at its height in Christ Jesus, in whom God perfectly manifested Himself and His ways with men. Christ is our Master and our Lord.[11] He is also meek and humble of heart.[12] And in attracting and inviting His disciples He acted patiently.[13] He wrought miracles to shed light on His teaching and to establish its truth. But His intention was to rouse faith in His hearers and to confirm them in faith, not to exert coercion upon them.[14]

He did indeed denounce the unbelief of some who listened to Him; but He left vengeance to God in expectation of the day of judgement.[15] When He sent His apostles into the world, He said to them: 'He who believes and is baptised shall be saved, but he who does not believe shall be condemned' (Mark 16:16); but He Himself, noting that cockle had been sown amid the wheat, gave orders that both should be allowed to grow until the harvest time, which will come at the end of the world.[16]

He refused to be a political Messiah, ruling by force;[17] He preferred to call Himself the Son of Man, who came 'to serve and to give his life as a ransom for many' (Mark 10:45). He showed Himself the perfect Servant of God:[18] 'a bruised reed he will not break, and a smoking wick he will not quench' (Matt. 12:20).

He acknowledged the power of government and its rights, when He commanded that tribute be

---

[11] Cf. Jn. 13:13.   [12] Cf. Mt. 11:29.
[13] Cf. Mt. 11:28–30; Jn. 6:67–68.
[14] Cf. Mt. 9:28–29; Mk. 9:23–24; 6, 5–6; Paul VI, encyclical *Ecclesiam Suam*, 6 August 1964: AAS 56 (1964), pp. 642–643.
[15] Cf. Mt. 11:20–24; Rom. 12: 19–20; 2 Th. 1:8.
[16] Cf. Mt. 13:30 and 40–42.   [17] Cf. Mt. 4:8–10; Jn. 6:15.
[18] Cf. Is. 42:1–4.

given to Caesar. But He gave clear warning that
the higher rights of God are to be kept inviolate:
'Render, therefore, to Caesar the things that are
Caesar's, and to God the things that are God's'
(Matt. 22:21).

In the end, when He completed on the cross the
work of redemption whereby He achieved salvation and true freedom for men, He also brought
His revelation to completion. He bore witness to
the truth,[19] but He refused to impose the truth by
force on those who spoke against it. Not by force
of blows does His rule assert its claims.[20] Rather,
it is established by witnessing to the truth and by
hearing the truth, and it extends its dominion by
the love whereby Christ, lifted up on the cross,
draws all men to Himself.[21]

Taught by the word and example of Christ, the
apostles followed the same way. From the very
origins of the Church the disciples of Christ strove
to convert men to faith in Christ as the Lord – not,
however, by the use of coercion or by devices unworthy of the gospel, but by the power, above all,
of the Word of God.[22] Steadfastly they proclaimed
to all the plan of God our Saviour, 'who wishes all
men to be saved and to come to the knowledge of
the truth' (1 Tim. 2:4). At the same time, however, they showed respect for weaker souls even
though these persons were in error. Thus they
made it plain that 'every one of us will render an
account of himself to God' (Rom. 14:12),[23] and
for this reason is bound to obey his conscience.

Like Christ Himself, the apostles were unceas-
ingly bent upon bearing witness to the truth of
God. They showed special courage in speaking

[19] Cf. Jn. 18:37.   [20] Cf. Mt. 26:51-53; Jn. 18:36.
[21] Cf. Jn. 12:32.   [22] Cf. 1 Cor. 2:3-5; 1 Th. 2:3-5.
[23] Cf. Rom. 14:1-23; 1 Cor. 8:9-13; 10:23-33.

'the word of God with boldness' (Acts 4:31)[24] before the people and their rulers. With a firm faith they held that the gospel is indeed the power of God unto salvation for all who believe.[25] Therefore they rejected all 'carnal weapons.'[26] They followed the example of the gentleness and respectfulness of Christ. And they preached the Word of God in the full confidence that there was resident in this Word itself a divine power able to destroy all the forces arrayed against God[27] and to bring men to faith in Christ and to His service.[28] As the Master, so too the apostles recognised legitimate civil authority. 'For there exists no authority except from God,' the Apostle teaches, and therefore commands: 'Let everyone be subject to the higher authorities . . . : he who resists the authority resists the ordinance of God' (Rom. 13:1-2).[29]

At the same time, however, they did not hesitate to speak out against governing powers which set themselves in opposition to the holy will of God: 'We must obey God rather than men' (Acts 5:29).[30] This is the way along which countless martyrs and other believers have walked through all ages and over all the earth.

12. The Church therefore is being faithful to the truth of the gospel, and is following the way of Christ and the apostles when she recognises, and gives support to, the principle of religious freedom as befitting the dignity of man and as being in accord with divine revelation. Throughout the ages, the Church has kept safe and handed on the

[24] Cf. Eph. 6:19-20.
[25] Cf. Rom. 1:16.
[26] Cf. 2 Cor. 10:4; 1 Th. 5:8-9.
[27] Cf. Eph. 6:11-17.
[28] Cf. 2 Cor. 10:3-5.
[29] Cf. 1 Pet. 2:13-17.
[30] Cf. Acts 4:19-20.

doctrine received from the Master and from the
apostles. In the life of the People of God as it has
made its pilgrim way through the vicissitudes of
human history, there have at times appeared ways
of acting which were less in accord with the spirit
of the gospel and even opposed to it. Nevertheless,
the doctrine of the Church that no one is to be
coerced into faith has always stood firm.

Thus the leaven of the gospel has long been
about its quiet work in the minds of men. To it is
due in great measure the fact that in the course of
time men have come more widely to recognise
their dignity as persons, and the conviction has
grown stronger that in religious matters the person.

13. Among the things which concern the good of the
Church and indeed the welfare of society here on
earth in society is to be kept free from all manner
of human coercion – things therefore which are always and everywhere to be kept secure and defended
against all injury – this certainly is pre-eminent,
namely, that the Church should enjoy that full
measure of freedom which her care for the salvation
of men requires.[31] This freedom is sacred, because
the only-begotten Son endowed with it the Church
which He purchased with His blood. It is so much
the property of the Church that to act against it is
to act against the will of God. The freedom of the
Church is the fundamental principle in what concerns the relations between the Church and
governments and the whole civil order.

In human society and in the face of government,
the Church claims freedom for herself in her

---

[31] Cf. Leo XIII, letter *Officio Sanctissimo*, 22 December 1887:
AAS 20 (1887), p. 269; idem, letter *Ex Litteris*, 7 April 1887:
AAS 19 (1886), p. 465.

character as a spiritual authority, established by Christ the Lord. Upon this authority there rests, by divine mandate, the duty of going out into the whole world and preaching the gospel to every creature.[32] The Church also claims freedom for herself in her character as a society of men who have the right to live in society in accordance with the precepts of Christian faith.[33]

In turn, where the principle of religious freedom is not only proclaimed in words or simply incorporated in law but also given sincere and practical application, there the Church succeeds in achieving a stable situation of right as well as of fact and the independence which is necessary for the fulfilment of her divine mission. This independence is precisely what the authorities of the Church claim in society.[34]

At the same time, the Christian faithful, in common with all other men, possess the civil right not to be hindered in leading their lives in accordance with their conscience. Therefore, a harmony exists between the freedom of the Church and the religious freedom which is to be recognised as the right of all men and communities and sanctioned by constitutional law.

14. In order to be faithful to the divine command, 'Make disciples of all nations' (Matt. 28:19), the Catholic Church must work with all urgency and concern 'that the Word of God may run and be glorified' (2 Thess. 3:1). Hence the Church

[32] Cf. Mk. 16:15; Mt. 28:18–20; Pius XII, encyclical *Summi Pontificatus*, 20 October 1939: AAS 31 (1939), pp. 445–446.
[33] Cf. Pius XI, letter *Firmissimam Constantiam*, 28 March 1937: AAS 29 (1937), p. 196.
[34] Cf. Pius XII, allocution *Ci Riesce*, 6 December 1953: AAS 45 (1953), p. 802.

earnestly begs of her children that, first of all, 'supplications, prayers, intercessions, and thanks-givings be made for all men. . . . For this is good and agreeable in the sight of God our Saviour, who wishes all men to be saved and to come to the knowledge of the truth' (1 Tim. 2:1–4).

In the formation of their consciences, the Christian faithful ought carefully to attend to the sacred and certain doctrine of the Church.[35] The Church is, by the will of Christ, the teacher of the truth. It is her duty to give utterance to, and authoritatively to teach, that Truth which is Christ Himself, and also to declare and confirm by her authority those principles of the moral order which have their origin in human nature itself. Furthermore, let Christians walk in wisdom in the face of those outside, 'in the Holy Spirit, in unaffected love, in the word of truth' (2 Cor. 6:6–7). Let them be about their task of spreading the light of life with all confidence[36] and apostolic courage, even to the shedding of their blood.

The disciple is bound by a grave obligation toward Christ his Master ever more adequately to understand the truth received from Him, faith-fully to proclaim it, and vigorously to defend it, never – be it understood – having recourse to means that are incompatible with the spirit of the gospel. At the same time, the charity of Christ urges him to act lovingly, prudently and patiently in his dealings with those who are in error or in ignorance with regard to the faith.[37] All is to be taken into account – the Christian duty to Christ, the life-

[35] Cf. Pius XII, radio message, 23 March 1952: AAS 44 (1952), pp. 270–278.

[36] Cf. Acts 4:29.

[37] Cf. John XXIII, encyclical *Pacem in Terris*, 11 April 1963: AAS 55 (1963), pp. 299–300.

giving Word which must be proclaimed, the rights of the human person, and the measure of grace granted by God through Christ to men, who are invited freely to accept and profess the faith.

15. The fact is that men of the present day want to be able freely to profess their religion in private and in public. Religious freedom has already been declared to be a civil right in most constitutions, and it is solemnly recognised in international documents.[38] The further fact is that forms of government still exist under which, even though freedom of religious worship receives constitutional recognition, the powers of government are engaged in the effort to deter citizens from the profession of religion and to make life difficult and dangerous for religious Communities.

This sacred Synod greets with joy the first of these two facts, as among the signs of the times. With sorrow, however, it denounces the other fact, as only to be deplored. The Synod exhorts Catholics, and it directs a plea to all men, most carefully to consider how greatly necessary religious freedom is, especially in the present condition of the human family.

All nations are coming into even closer unity. Men of different cultures and religions are being brought together in closer relationships. There is a growing consciousness of the personal responsibility that weighs upon every man. All this is evident.

Consequently, in order that relationships of peace and harmony may be established and maintained within the whole of mankind, it is necessary that religious freedom be everywhere provided

[38] Cf. John XXIII, encyclical *Pacem in Terris,* 11 April 1963: AAS 55 (1963), pp. 295–296.

with an effective constitutional guarantee, and that respect be shown for the high duty and right of man freely to lead his religious life in society.

May the God and Father of all grant that the human family, through careful observance of the principle of religious freedom in society, may be brought by the grace of Christ and the power of the Holy Spirit to the sublime and unending 'freedom of the glory of the sons of God' (Rom. 8:21).

Each and every one of the things set forth in this Declaration has won the consent of the Fathers of this most sacred Council. We too, by the apostolic authority conferred on us by Christ, join with the Venerable Fathers in approving, decreeing, and establishing these things in the Holy Spirit, and we direct that what has thus been enacted in synod be published to God's glory.

Rome, at St Peter's, 7 December 1965
I, Paul, Bishop of the Catholic Church

There follow the signatures of the Fathers.

3. A Commentary on the Declaration

The title of this document, *A Declaration on Religious Freedom; on the right of the person and communities to social and civil freedom in matters religious*, is an indication of its intention and scope. The term tolerance, implying acceptance of a necessary evil, does not occur. In its title at least the declaration of Vatican II makes a clean break with the thesis-hypothesis approach which had dominated so much recent Catholic writing. This is evidently not intended to be a concession *in fact* combined with a denial in theory or in the ideal. The concern is with the 'right of the person and communities to social and civil freedom in matters religious' and, as the text makes clear, the title has to be taken as it stands, involving a genuine right of every person and every community, without invoking the two standards enshrined in the thesis-hypothesis teaching.

The description of the document as a declaration distinguishes it in authority from other documents issued by the Council, called constitutions or decrees. The precise effect of these distinctions is not very clear. Because of the centrality of the subjects discussed, the theological depth at which they were discussed and the comprehensiveness of the final statement, the constitutions, at least the dogmatic constitutions on the Church and on Divine Revelation, may have been distinguished from all others. They are certainly given the most authoritative title. Yet in keeping with the pastoral aims of the Council and the explicit intentions of the Pope and of all the Council fathers, these documents are not given such definitive status that they could be described as infallible. They are issued by the supreme authority of the Church demanding our full adherence as the Church's authentic understanding of Christ's message in these areas.

The *Declaration on Religious Freedom* lacks the finality of an infallible statement as well as the doctrinal depth and comprehensiveness of the other documents mentioned above. Yet it takes its rightful place in Catholic teaching as an authoritative expression of the Church's understanding of the meaning, basis and extent of man's personal right to freedom in religious matters, whether acting as an individual or in society. It marks a decisive stage in the development of this understanding and indicates the way of future development.

Introduction

It is some measure of the listening and learning attitude which characterised the present Council that it should begin this Declaration by calling attention to two preoccupations of contemporary man – 'a sense of the dignity of the human person' and the need for 'constitutional limits . . . to the powers of government'.

It is not sufficiently realised within or without the Church how dependent Christian teachers and thinkers must be on the intellectual movements of their own time, how preoccupied they must be with the human problems of their time. In itself this dependence and this preoccupation is neither good nor bad, simply inevitable. What may be good or bad are the attitudes and practical reactions which the dependence and preoccupation provoke. In the past, due to human weakness and sin which the Church must always bear within it, there have been some unfortunate if understandable attitudes and reactions of both acceptance and rejection of contemporary ideas. In the manner and style of exercising authority for example, the Church has been influenced by the prevailing secular manner and style. The prince-bishops, the 'my lord', the ring and mitre, the palace, the non-dialogical and unparticipated exclusiveness of episcopal or papal authority are not pure deduction from the evangelical character of Church authority but to some extent reflections of practice current at various times amongst contemporary secular authorities. And it is difficult to say whether the Church has suffered more from the mistakes of uncritical acceptance or uncritical rejection in the face of contemporary ideas and problems. Yet face them it must. And as human reason and human values are by the Church's own revealed teaching means and reflections of the ultimate divine truth and must be in continuous state of development due to man's historical character, the attitude should be one of critical appreciation. It is by such critical appreciation in the past that Christianity has renewed itself and shown its vitality in successive intellectual and political climates. No list of mistakes can obscure the fact of its survival and not simply as a relic but as a continuing vital influence.

What is striking about the opening phrases of this Declaration is the attitude of humble if critical appraisal and that in a matter in which churchmen of recent times were not accustomed to listen humbly. The desire of men for freedom, freedom to develop responsibly as persons in society, and the corresponding demand for limitation on the powers of government are singled out amongst the aspirations of modern man and declared to be 'greatly in accord with truth and justice'. In support of this declaration the Church proposes to draw on its resources of revealed doctrine and human reflection through the centuries. Whatever the concrete form of political organisation, the freedom of the person particularly 'in the quest for the values proper to the human spirit' and the limitation of the powers of government so necessary to this freedom (which practically comprise basic democracy) are recognised by the Church here as definite and irreversible advances in man's ordering of society. Many régimes of the present and recent past could not, using these criteria, be described as 'in accord with truth and justice'.

It is worth noting that the 'limitations of government' element did not appear in earlier versions. Its introduction may be taken to mark the growing influence of Father Courtney Murray's ideas, which are so evident in the document, particularly in the first section.

To allay the fears of some critics that a declaration on religious freedom would give the impression that the Church was abandoning its claims, the Council professes its belief that God has made known the one true religion and that this 'subsists in the Catholic and Apostolic Church', and that all men are bound to seek and hold the truth especially in regard to religion. This section of paragraph 1 does not appear here in the earlier drafts or elsewhere at such great length. It was introduced to mollify the opponents of the declaration by removing the alleged danger that by supporting religious freedom the Church might appear to be abandoning its claims and admitting that one religion was as good as another. In the event it made no difference to the opposition's attitude which was maintained to the very end. It adds little clarification to the document itself which in its later exposition of what it means by religious freedom rules out any notion of indifferentism. It has been criticised by some as unecumenical but the doctrinal position is undeniably Catholic and the phraseology ('subsists in') was hailed as ecumenical in the documents from which it was taken – the constitution *On the Church* and the decree *On Ecumenism*. Whether it is wise to stress the obvious may be doubted but the addition makes no real difference to the declaration.

More difficult to interpret is the statement shortly after, that religious freedom as concerned 'with immunity in civil society therefore leaves untouched the traditional Catholic doctrine on the moral duty of men and societies towards the true religion and toward the one Church of Christ'.

The part concerned with the moral duty of the individual is clear enough. That on the moral duty of societies is another matter. The recent controversy in the Church on religious freedom which this declaration tries to resolve, seemed inextricably bound up with a wider controversy on the relations between Church and State, between Church and society. To say that the traditional Catholic doctrine on the duty of societies to the Church remains untouched itself leaves untouched the question as to what must be regarded as traditional Catholic doctrine. The teaching of the manuals on 'public ecclesiastical law' on the matter can hardly be regarded as pure Catholic doctrine. What is certain is that this doctrine must incorporate the teaching of Vatican II on religious liberty.

The final sentence of paragraph 1 outlines the document's approach to religious freedom by developing 'the doctrine of recent Popes on the inviolable rights of the human person and on the constitutional order of society'.

The Meaning of the Right to Religious Freedom

Because of the obscurity, even ambiguity, of previous Church statements in this matter, as recent controversy had indicated, it was necessary to have a clear, unambiguous declaration of the right of the human person to religious freedom. This the present Council provides in the opening sentence of paragraph 2, 'This Vatican Council declares that the human person has a right to religious freedom'. And the freedom is defined as 'immunity from coercion' by individuals or societies in religious matters. This immunity means that he may never be forced by any human power to act contrary to his conscience and that he enjoys freedom to act in accordance with it, 'within due limits'. The range of the freedom and the due limits are worked out later in the document but the essential declaration cannot be challenged and is unparalleled in the Church's earlier statements. The community's understanding of itself and its mission, of the human person and of the world in which we live to-day, so evidently growing throughout Vatican II, has enabled it to approve religious liberty in principle as a human right and not as a concession to *force majeure*. The necessary limitations to which the exercise of this as of all human rights is subject cannot weaken the force of this basic statement of principle.

It is important, of course, to understand what is being affirmed as religious freedom. It is not the right of the individual to freedom from God or from the obligations of the religion in which God reveals Himself. Such a right would be an absurdity. The right to religious freedom is concerned with human relationships. It is the individual human being's right to seek the truth about himself, his destiny, God, free from coercion by any other human power, whether individual or social. It is this immunity in relation to other human beings which is in question.

It has both negative and positive aspects. Negatively it means that a man may not be forced to believe or act contrary to his conscience by any human authority. This is an elementary truth of the Christian faith, accepted from the beginning, although it was sometimes obscured in theory even by such minds as those of St Augustine and St Thomas, and ignored in practice by Christian Emperors and Catholic and Protestant Princes. Its best known recent formulation was that of Canon 1351 of the Code of Canon Law: *Ad amplerandam fidem catholicam nemo invitus cogatur* – 'Nobody may be forced to embrace the Catholic faith against his will'.

But religious liberty demands some freedom of action for the subject. And the immunity which it grants means, according to the document, that a man may not be prevented from acting in accordance with his conscience 'within due limits'. This expression is definitely superior to the most explicit statement on the matter previously issued by the Church, that of Pope John XXIII in his encyclical *Peace on Earth*: 'Every human being has the right to honour God according to the sincere dictates of conscience (*ad rectam conscientiae suae normam*) and therefore the right to worship God publicly and privately'. It would be impossible to deny that the whole context of this encyclical plus the words used strongly support what is unequivocally affirmed by Vatican II. Yet the interpretation of 'sincere' or 'upright conscience' could lead to difficulties which the new document skilfully avoids. And the statement here dispenses forever with the tolerance for a greater good, the old thesis-hypothesis approach, in favour of a human right which remains valid, as is later stated, even if there is culpable failure in its exercise, so that the conscience involved is neither true (*vera*) nor upright (*recta*).

As it is a right in relation to other human beings, it will be exercised and must be protected in society. For this legal guarantee is necessary so that what is a human right becomes a civil right. The Council's determination to promote religious freedom could hardly be more effectively demonstrated than by its demand that it be recognised in the constitutional law of each society and so become a civil right. Its refusal at the same time to adopt the suggestion of some Fathers that it speak only of a civil right demonstrates its understanding of the true basis of religious freedom in man's endowment as a person and makes it superior to governments and civil laws, which do not grant it but recognise and guarantee it.

The Basis of the Right

One of the great stumbling-blocks in the development of an understanding of religious freedom has been the dispute about its basis. This dispute has certainly been aggravated by the use of such slogans as 'error has no rights' or 'error may not enjoy the same rights as truth'. Once this frame of reference is adopted the only satisfactory conclusion is repression of error in principle or in *thesi*, with tolerance possible in practice or *in hypothesi*. The frame is in fact an unreal one because rights belong to persons not to abstractions such as truth or error.

However, the problem still remains, it seems, as to whether persons in error may enjoy equal rights with those who accept the truth, whether these persons have the right openly to profess error and to propagate it. Here again there is need for further precision in regard to right. Only persons enjoy rights and they enjoy them only in relation to other persons, whether as individuals or as organised in society. The right of religious freedom then is a right in relation to others and, as the declaration states, it consists precisely in an immunity. What right to religious freedom involves in relation to other human beings and all human authority is an immunity from coercion in religious matters. It is not a right in relation to the personal God, to ignore or reject Him or His religion.

This immunity from coercion is demanded by man's personal dignity as a knowing, free being who is naturally and morally bound to seek the truth, to adhere to it as he sees it and to live by it. To do this properly he must enjoy not only psychological freedom but immunity from coercion. The right does not depend on his own subjective dispositions but on his objective nature and dignity which are good and true in themselves. The right is therefore not founded on evil or error.

The foundation of the right to religious liberty in the objective order of man's personal nature has many theoretical and practical advantages. It escapes the artificial difficulties raised by 'the error has no rights' school by concentrating on the person as source of rights. It escapes the more real difficulties connected with attempts to found the right in the demands of a sincere, upright conscience (*conscientia recta*) even if it is false. This raises first of all the problem about how a person's right to do something can be derived from a false understanding of reality even if it is sincere. There is the further problem of distinguishing between sincere and insincere conscience judgements. Who does this and how? And finally there will remain the unenviable discrimination between the sincere and insincere. These last two difficulties are certainly insoluble in practice as the first may well be insoluble in theory.

The Declaration does not base the right on any false understanding of reality in relation to a particular action but on a true understanding of the person in relation to a general immunity. The right is to an immunity from interference by others, in particular by the State, the lawful and actual possessor of coercive power in society. And this immunity belongs to everyone because of his human nature, whether his grasp of reality is true or false, whether he lives up to his obligation of seeking it honestly or not.

The argument advanced here has the further merit of providing a very broad basis for agreement between men and societies. Its only presupposition is man in his freedom and capacity for the truth, a presupposition that is at least widely accepted in practice. As the declaration is anxious for the widest possible acceptance of the right and to have the moral right transformed into a civil right everywhere, this method of argumentation is important. Perhaps its one possible disadvantage is that its insistence on the objective foundation of the right in human nature aggravates the historical difficulties created by previous Church statements particularly in the nineteenth century.

The argument is developed in the succeeding paragraph 3 in a number of important ways. The knowing, free nature of man with his commitment to the truth is traced back to the eternal plan or law of God in which man now participates freely. Here the points made previously are given the sanction of divine law and the immunity which man enjoys is specifically related to his obligation to his freedom to seek religious truth. This obligation must be fulfilled by each man personally and yet in society. The personal obligation and responsibility only takes shape in social activity. All man's search for truth has a necessary social dimension so that he must work in co-operation and exchange with other men if he is personally to understand and adhere to the truth. 'The enquiry must be free, carried on with the aid of teaching or instruction, communication and dialogue, in the course of which men explain to each other the truth they have discovered or think they have discovered, in order thus to assist one another in the quest for truth.'(§3). The social exchange no less than the personal freedom is essential to man's characteristic seach for the truth, including religious truth, and should enjoy the same immunity. This should dispose once and for all of the alleged conflict between truth and freedom. As Bishop Ancel so effectively pointed out in the Council, they are inseparably joined together in man who can only seek and accept the truth in freedom.

All this may be expressed slightly differently if one recognises that man's understanding of that reality called divine law is mediated through his conscience, so that he must enjoy immunity from human coercion in regard to the formation of his conscience judgements. He may never be compelled to act against them and he may not be prevented from acting in accordance with them within certain limits essential to the survival of society.[1] This applies especially to religious matters, the document continues, because religious acts are first of all 'internal, voluntary and free acts' by which man is related to God and these acts are beyond reach of all human authority. However, as a result of his social nature, he must give external expression to these internal acts, he must seek and profess religious truth socially so that this immunity applies over the whole range of his religious activity, provided the necessary limits are observed,

[1] Quoted in *The Tablet*, 2 October 1965, 1106.

described here now for the first time as 'the just requirements of public order'.

To emphasise the reality of this social immunity still more, paragraph 3 concludes by pointing out that man's religious reality and activity transcend the order of 'terrestrial and temporal realities' for which government and civil law accept some responsibility and have a certain competence. And while government should in the interests of the common welfare recognise and favour the religious life of the citizenry, 'it would clearly transgress the limits set to its power were it to presume to command or inhibit acts that are religious'.

This is a consequence of the dual order of authority and society which is suggested by Christ's 'Render to Caesar' and realised by His foundation of a Church that would be a visible society with responsibility for man's religious life and yet distinct, in a way unknown to His Jewish and Greco-Roman contemporaries, from the civil society or State. It marks a radical characteristic of Christianity which has now passed into the recognised political heritage of Europe and the Western World and is becoming more accepted elsewhere, if not always for the same reasons. The implications of the distinction have been obscured, exaggerated and distorted by churchmen and politicians in the course of history. The implications themselves are necessarily conditioned by the historical situation which may differ quite a bit in different countries at the same time as well as in the same country at different times. However, for both secular and religious reasons, the distinction is growing gradually clearer to-day and becoming more consistently applicable due to the slow but growing unity of the world. It was the reassertion of this distinction in forthright terms by Leo XIII that set the stage for the development in the Church's understanding of itself, of man and the secular world which culminated in this declaration, amongst other things. And despite certain obscurities, some inevitably due to the historical dimension of the Church's existence and some due to inadequate analysis of the realities involved – Church, State, community and person – the Council's clear statement on religious freedom marks a decisive step forward in the acceptance by churchmen of the distinction between Church and State and of the limitations of each.

The Range of the Right

The discussion of the right to religious freedom and of its foundation has made clear the social dimension of the right, that it involves an immunity in regard to external and social acts as well as internal ones. This aspect receives a fuller treatment in the succeeding paragraphs 4 and 5.

The immunity men enjoy as individuals must also be recognised in their community activity because of man's social nature and that of religion. This immunity, within the just limits of public order, applies to all religious communities in regard to social worship, internal organisation, religious instruction and education of their own members and ministers, religious institutions of various kinds, the ownership and administration of property, public preaching and spread of their doctrine and way of life. Religious freedom implies also the freedom 'to show the special value of their doctrine in what concerns the organisation of society and the inspiration of the whole of human activity'. This applies to all religious groups and is a right to demonstrate or show to others the special value of their doctrine for society, not of course to impose it. How conflicting doctrines or the organisation of social life may be resolved is ultimately a political problem but its solution may not destroy this element of the right to religious freedom.

The family receives special attention in paragraph 5 as a participant in man's social right to religious freedom. It has 'the right freely to live its own domestic religious life under the guidance of parents'. The point of the paragraph would seem to be, however, the right of parents to determine the religious education of their children and their right 'in consequence', as the Declaration puts it, 'to make a genuinely free choice of schools and of other means of education'. And it would be unjust to impose extra burdens on people who use this freedom, while the rights of the parents to religious freedom would be violated by compelling their children to attend 'lessons not in agreement with their religious beliefs, or if a single system of education, from which all religious education is excluded, is imposed upon all'.

The reference to education did not appear in earlier versions and was introduced at the suggestion of Cardinal Conway of Armagh amongst others. The relations between religious and general education and so between the parents' rights as exercised through the Church or religious community and the State are badly in need of elucidation. It is very doubtful if the Council's document on *Christian Education* contributed much to this. It is undoubtedly true, as paragraph 5 of the Religious Freedom document asserts, that parents have the primary rights and that they are violated by enforced instruction contrary to the beliefs of the child. But whether there may be other legitimate alternatives to Church schools, according to the circumstances of time and place, requires fuller discussion.

The Responsibility for Religious Freedom

As further evidence of how far the Council has absorbed the democratic consciousness of our own day, it declares that the responsibility for 'the care of the right to religious freedom devolves' first of all 'upon the whole citizenry', then 'upon social groups, upon government, upon the Church and other religious communities'. This responsibility derives from their duty to the common welfare which 'chiefly consists in the protection of the rights, and in the performance of the duties, of the human person'. (It is perhaps a pity that amongst the social groups or institutions the press was not singled out as the responsible and effective guardian of freedom in religious as in other matters which it can be and frequently is.)

The protection and promotion of religious freedom amongst inviolable human rights is an essential duty of government, of the supreme political and legal authorities in society. The human right must become a civil right, enjoying the protection of the law and the courts. (The government's duty to favour religious life amongst the citizens so that society may profit from 'the moral qualities of peace and justice' gets a passing mention here.)

The promotion and protection of religious freedom demands the equality of all citizens before the law. No discrimination, open or covert, on religious grounds may be practised. And of course the imposition on the citizens of the profession or the repudiation of any religion by law, or their hindrance in joining or leaving a religious community or the forcible repression of all religion would be clear violations of the human right. The different elements of religious liberty which should be protected by law according to this paragraph correspond closely to Article 18 of the United Nations Declaration of Human Rights,

Article 9 of the European Convention for Human
Rights and Article 44 of the Irish Constitution
amongst contemporary political documents.

The paragraph also makes allowance for the situation where, due to historical circumstances, one
religion is given 'special legal recognition' in a particular society, such as may be found for Christian
Churches in Spain and Britain, and for others in
Africa and Asia. Such recognition is not of itself a
violation of religious liberty but 'it is at the same time
imperative that the right of all citizens and religious
communities to religious freedom should be recognised and made effective in practice'.

The Limitations of the Right

The right to religious freedom is a right to be exercised in society. It has therefore certain necessary
limitations imposed by the nature of human society.
If these limitations are not respected, social life breaks
down and the exercise of human rights becomes
impossible. This is the subject of paragraph 7.

These limitations are firstly moral limitations. As
the right is primarily a human, moral right, it bears
with it its own responsibilities. In exercise of his right
each man must respect the rights of the others and the
general social welfare. His approach to others should
be founded in the charity all men owe each other, be
continually sensitive to the demands of truth and
justice. In an earlier section (paragraph 4) dealing
with the right to propagate one's religion, the
Declaration warns against the use of unfair means.
Deliberate dishonesty in one's presentation of religion
or offers of material gain in connection with it are
personal abuses of one's own freedom and violations
of another no less than fear or force. Such methods

might be called proselytism as distinct from missionary activity and condemned as unworthy of Christianity or any serious religion.

Just as the moral right demands legal recognition, so do its limitations, that people may be able to live in harmony in society and exercise their rights. The laws then protecting the right to religious freedom must also lay down the limits to what may be done in the name of religious freedom. These limits, however, are aimed ultimately at protection of all the citizens in the free exercise of this and other rights, at providing means of settling conflicts that might arise, at ensuring the necessary public peace in society through due order and justice and finally 'out of the need for a proper guardianship of public morality'. Together these three elements form an important part of the common good or welfare of political society and they are described in the document as constituting that part of the common welfare known as 'public order'. Religious liberty is therefore limited by the due requirements of public order which means respect for the rights of others, public peace and public morality. Here the Declaration follows the line of the European Convention and the Irish Constitution.[2] It favours the expression of these limitations in law, as the European Convention insists. But lest advantage be taken of this 'escape' clause to curtail genuine freedom, it retains as the fundamental guiding principle 'the freedom of man

[2] European Convention for the Protection of Human Rights. Art. 9, §2: 'Freedom to manifest one's religion or beliefs shall be subject only to such limitations as are prescribed by law and are necessary in a democratic society in the interests of public safety, for the protection of public order, health or morals, or for the protection of the rights and freedom of others.' Constitution of Ireland. Art. 44, §2.10: 'Freedom of conscience and the free profession and practice of religion are, subject to public order and morality, guaranteed to every citizen.'

is to be respected as far as possible and is not to be curtailed except when and in so far as necessary'.

The crucial question of how public morality is to be determined is not tackled and it could not be expected to be. But there is no doubt that much of the difficulty of implementing the Declaration may be concerned with this. Some comments on the problem are given elsewhere in this book although the debate has become more defined in Britain, at least since these comments were written, by the publications of Professor Hart and Lord Devlin.[3]

The final paragraph 8 in the first major part of the Declaration urges the need for education to responsible freedom. Recognition of religious freedom should contribute to the general growth of responsibility so that each man gradually assumes personal responsibility before God and society for his activity and uses this responsibility to promote truth and justice and charity in freedom. In this direction the progress possible is indefinite, and moral or juridical limitations have no place.

The Lesson of Revelation

In understanding the dignity of man and its moral demands, the Christian is not, of course, dependent solely on the reflection and experience of mankind. God's manifestation of Himself in revelation which was addressed to man revealed a great deal about man himself. And one of the most obvious and important of these was the respect for human freedom which God maintained in all His dealings with man. This was fully exemplified by Christ in addressing Himself to man, as God become man. Divine

[3] H. L. A. Hart, *Law, Liberty and Morality*, Oxford. Patrick Devlin, *The Enforcement of Morals*, Oxford, 1965.

revelation is the self-communication of God which reached its climax in Christ. But this self-communication is really an invitation to man to accept and to accept freely a loving union with the divine. That immunity from human coercion which is strictly speaking religious freedom is not explicitly mentioned in the scriptures, as the Declaration admits, but it has its roots there in the understanding of that dignity which man as the free recipient of the divine invitation enjoys. The dignity and the freedom are strongly evident in the freedom of the act of faith, as evident from the New Testament as well as the attitude and activities of Christ and His apostles in offering the invitation to men on behalf of the Father (paragraph 9).

Paragraph 10 develops the notion of the freedom of the act of faith. Freedom is of the essence of man's response in faith to the divine invitation. This is the clear doctrine of revelation and the constant teaching of the Church. This freedom is, of course, eliminated by coercion where a man is forced to profess some belief. And it is obscured and diminished below the human level where he is prevented from externally professing and acting on his conscientious beliefs. The principle of religious freedom as proposed by Vatican II is intended to ensure the genuine exercise of that freedom 'by the creation of an environment in which men can without hindrance be invited to Christian faith, embrace it of their own free will, and profess it effectively in their whole manner of life'.

The freedom of the act of faith emerges most clearly in God's call as it was manifested in Christ (paragraph 10). The true worshippers of God who would serve Him in spirit and in truth are morally obliged to follow Christ in His 'Come after me', but any suggestion of physical coercion would be clearly opposed to the teaching and example of the Master.

There is much greater consciousness in the Church today of Christ as the central mystery dominating not only our faith and prayer but also our activity and so the theology of that activity, moral theology.

To live as Christ lived, to behave to ohters as Christ behaved to them, to see every action as a fulfilment of the two great commandments of love, to treat Christ not only as the model and teacher but also in His own person and being as the standard or norm of morality, these are the growing tendencies in the movement to renew moral theology.[4] With such a Christ-centred, love-structured system of morality the manoeuvring for political privilege for the Church and Christianity through discrimination against others becomes unthinkable. The Declaration naturally does not develop a complete morality of Christian behaviour. It does, however, invoke in this spirit the example and teaching of Christ in His preaching of the kingdom, a lead which all Christians must follow. This involves the unqualified recognition of man's freedom in regard to the invitation, the rejection of all coercion, toleration of the cockle amongst the wheat until the final harvesting and the radical distinction of His kingdom from any political kingdom. The principle of religious liberty ensures in a most effective way the possibility of continuing Christ's preaching in Christ's manner. Any violation of it in His name would be double treason to both the message and the manner.

The Acts of the Apostles and the various letters of St Paul and the others show how faithful these first preachers remained to the mission of their Master in this respect (paragraph 12). They preached the Gospel that each man might accept it freely because

---

[4] Cf. McDonagh (Ed.), *Moral Theology Renewed*, Dublin, 1966.

each must ultimately give an account of himself and so must obey his conscience. All 'carnal weapons' are ruled out and their trust is in the Word of God and its power to open men's hearts.

Both Christ and His Apostles recognised the power of legitimate civil authority and man's duty to obey it but it must be held distinct from and ultimately subordinate to God's word and its freedom.

In all this the Church has had no choice except to follow Christ and His immediate disciples. So despite the obscurities and ambiguities of history, the failures in practice of Christian princes and church-men, the failures in reflexion and expression of Christian teachers, it has held on to the principle that no one may be coerced into the faith. The present Declaration enables it to propose in fuller and more Christian terms the complete implications of this principle after the mind and manner of Christ and His Apostles (paragraph 12).

Having discussed the principle's roots in revelation, the Declaration shows how religious freedom har-monises with what it calls 'the fundamental principle in what concerns the relations between the Church and governments and the whole civil order' (para-graph 13). This is an important element in the argument because one of the objections to the Declaration was that the recognition of freedom of religion for all necessarily involved some inhibition of the Church's freedom, by exposing people to error as well as truth. But, of course, Christ and His Apostles never claimed more for themselves than that they be given a hearing. Their trust was not in the elimination of competition but in the power of God's Word of Truth. The Church is called to fulfil its mission in the same inevitable human conditions by introducing the Word of God to men groping for truth and only partially finding and communicating

it. This can only be done in the freedom from State
or other human coercion proclaimed here. The full
observance of this principle enables the Church to be
what she is and to live 'as a society of men who have
the right to live in society in accordance with the
precepts of the Christian faith' (paragraph 13).

The freedom of the Church argument is important
here for another reason. It gives a historical link with
the early claims of the Church as formulated in the
second century by Lactantuus and Tertullian,
elaborated later and developed above all in the
controversial nineteenth century by Leo XIII. So
Father Murray could say that the fundamental principle governing Church-State relations for Leo was
that now explicitly said to be so by this Declaration,
the freedom of the Church. In this further development of the teaching on Church-State relations this
statement will naturally be very important.

Paragraph 13 on the freedom of the Church concludes by emphasising that the stable situation provided by legal guarantee of religious liberty satisfies
the claims of the Church in society and enables it to
carry out its mission.

The following paragraph deals with the Church's
urgent mission to the world, which is to preach the
Word of Christ in the freedom contemplated. And
it is the task of all Christians. However, that they
may fully understand, live and so communicate it
they must attend to the 'sacred and certain doctrine
of the Church'. And they must never invoke unworthy means.

In conclusion, paragraph 14 summarises the elements which must be taken into account in the
Christian's discharge of his mission: 'The Christian
duty to Christ, the life-giving Word which must be
proclaimed and the rights of human person, and the
measure of grace granted by God through Christ to

men, who are invited freely to accept and profess the faith'.

Conclusion

The final paragraph 15 opens by recounting two facts of the contemporary world. The first, a matter for rejoicing, is the desire of men freely to profess and practise their religion in public and private and the recognition of this as a civil right in many states and by international documents. The second, a matter for regret, is the effective denial of this freedom in so many countries. Here the Declaration accepts fully the present-day understanding and practice of religious freedom as it is enshrined in documents like the United Nations Declaration on Human Rights, the European Convention, the first Amendment to the American Constitution and Article forty-four of the Irish Constitution. In its reference to States in which religious freedom is denied it is thinking, of course, of certain Communist régimes but also of some Western régimes where Catholics and Protestants discriminate in law and in fact against each other. The Council 'exhorts' Catholics and 'directs a plea to all men' to recognise the necessity of religious freedom today. The growing and necessary unity of mankind makes it essential to peace and harmony among men. Their temporal and spiritual development requires 'that religious freedom be everywhere provided with an effective constitutional guarantee and that respect be shown for the high duty and right of man freely to lead his religious life in society'.

The Declaration closes with a prayer that the Father may bring all 'through careful observance of the principle of religious freedom' to enjoy 'the glorious freedom of the sons of God'. So despite the chequered history of the document and its remaining obscurities Vatican II has in this Declaration given one striking indication of internal renewal as a step to promoting the Church's relationships with other Christians and all men of good will by firmly and clearly advocating the moral and civil right of all to religious freedom. Even five years ago it would have been considered almost impossible to achieve this now, ten years ago impossible. But the Church remains full of surprises as the Council has demonstrated. And what is impossible to man remains possible to God.

4. The Conciliar Context of the Declaration

The History of the Declaration

The chequered history of the Declaration is quite well known. The moves and countermoves in promoting and opposing it were reported avidly in the world press. For some Council fathers, as well as interested observers within and without the Council chamber, it became a symbol of the success or failure of the Council. For the leaders of what gradually became the reforming majority and still more for the leaders of the 'no change' minority, the issue of religious freedom was crucial. From its first introduction in the second session in November 1963 as the fifth chapter of the *schema* on ecumenism it met with the most enthusiastic support and the bitterest opposition. There was serious disappointment when it was prevented from being put to the first preliminary vote at this session. Despite aged Cardinal Bea's reassurance that it was only lack of time which had caused this, and that the document on religious freedom was merely postponed, it supporters were worried lest what was almost certainly the will of the majority would be thwarted by the manoeuvres of a powerful and organised minority.

The third session witnessed a new setting for the document. It appeared first in September as an appendix to the *schema* on ecumenism and was the occasion of some very sharp discussion. In November it reappeared as a separate and thoroughly revised document, prepared again by the Secretariat for Unity and equipped with a Nihil Obstat from the Theological Commission and a mixed commission which had been suggested in a now famous letter from Cardinal Cigognani to the Secretariat for Unity on 17 October and which had sparked off one of the several crises at the third session. A very strong letter signed by seventeen cardinals and addressed to the Pope personally prevented what seemed to be a move effectively to withdraw the drafting of the declaration from the Secretariat and give the leaders of the minority group a much greater say in its formulation. The new version however provided occasion for further high drama since despite announcements of a vote at this session the vote was postponed at the request of a group of bishops who wished to have further time to study it. This last announcement in the closing days of the session stung the main supporters of the Declaration into unprecedented action. They collected over four hundred signatures to a petition addressed to the Pope to have a vote taken, and the petition was taken by Cardinals Meyer, Leger and Ritter to the Pope from the Council hall. The Pope however accepted the decision of the presidential council against a vote as in accordance with the rules of procedure. Cardinal Tisserant added that the *schema* would be examined at the following session and if possible before all others.

And so it was. The fourth and final session opened in September 1965 with a debate on a further revised *schema*. The debate followed the well-worn pattern, evoking very loud minority opposition. Again there was a crisis about the voting. But at the direction of the Pope, the vote was finally taken on 22 September with 1997 approving substantially of the *schema*, 224 against and one null vote. The Council had finally committed itself and committed itself massively to the principle of religious freedom. The Secretariat of Unity had a mandate to continue its work. The final version which included a more explicit and developed reference to the 'one Church of Christ' and men's obligation to it, received final conciliar endorsement but met with the same hard core of opposition. From Vatican II there emerged a basically clear and very welcome statement on the freedom of each man to seek the truth as an individual in society and to live according to it. The many critical moments on the way had made the final achievement all the more satisfying and the persistence and intelligence of the opposition gave the declaration a bite and solidity that it might have otherwise missed.

Relation to the Council's Programme

Set beside the physical size and intellectual scope of many of the other documents of Vatican II, the Declaration on religious freedom seems slight. Was it really a peripheral issue at the Council which perhaps for historical reasons and reasons of personalities was treated in exaggerated fashion by the Council fathers and the press? Were the successive crises it provoked out of proportion to what was at stake and to what actually emerged? Where did it fit into the programme of the Council in the aggiornamento with a view to reunion of Pope John or the more self-consciously developed programme of Pope Paul, the self-awareness and renewal of the Church as a way to dialogue with other Christians and with the world? If it did fit in, had it an important role? The full answers to these questions will only gradually take shape as the work begun by the Council is carried on by the whole Church. It is possible, however, and important to indicate the answers suggested by the Council decrees themselves.

The Self-knowledge and Renewal of the Church

In the task of self-knowledge and renewal, the major achievements of the Council were undoubtedly the Dogmatic Constitutions, *On the Church*, *On Revelation* and *On the Sacred Liturgy*. By these two documents the developments in the Church's understanding of itself prepared by the biblical, theological and spiritual movements of recent decades were critically examined, synthesised and given official approval.

One of the primary insights into the nature of the Church to be derived from these documents is the sacramental or 'mystery' character of the Church. Chapter 1 of *On the Church* is called 'The Mystery of the Church'. And recent theology has described the Church as the 'Sacrament of Christ' as Christ was the 'Sacrament of God'. Here sacrament is being used analogically, yet not equivocally and means an effective sign of God's presence, both signifying the presence of God and effecting or realising it. Christ the God-man was the climax to all signs of the divine presence with mankind and achieved that presence in the fullest possible way. In the original and complete sense Jesus Christ is *Revelation*, the Word of God to man (*On Revelation*, Ch. 1). His work of mediating God to man and man to God in sign and reality, completed at the Resurrection, was continued in the world by the community which He founded while on earth and brought to completion by the gift of the Spirit at Pentecost.

As the sign and effective means of God's saving presence to man in the world, the Church is also the sign of the unity of mankind. It is as called by the Father in Christ through the gift of the Spirit that all men are ultimately and intimately united with each other. So the moral demands enshrined in God's communication of Himself to man are summed up in the two great precepts, love of God and love of fellow-man. Unity with God and with each other are inseparable parts of the one response demanded by this divine presence amongst us.

The presence itself is made visible in a people. Chapter 2 of *On the Church* is entitled 'On the People of God'. It marks a further important stage in the Church's self-understanding. God's presence to man is a personal call to union with Him addressed to each man. In His saving plan however this presence has been mediated through a people, the people of Israel in the old agreement or covenant between God and man and the new people of God, the new Israel in the new covenant. It is in and through a people that the divine presence achieved in Christ as God become man, is visibly signified and realised.

And this people of His is the community of the called (the *qahal*, the *ecclesia*). The call or invitation is free as the response is free. The invited and responding constitute a people through the power of the divine presence in Christ embodying the invitation and empowering the response. Scattered, divided men turned in on themselves are opened up to each other by being opened up to their common Father in Christ through the Spirit, who is given to them. By receiving the Spirit of sonship, they become sons indeed of the Father, brothers of Christ and of each other. The divinely established personal bonds that unite them with the three divine persons inevitably unite them with each other. And as mem-

bers of God's people they enjoy a basic equality
which no differentiation of task or function may
obscure. In the life and mission of that people as
signifying and mediating God's love and presence to
all men they are fully involved.

To promote the life of the people in truth and in
loving unity, a special ministry or service was instituted by Christ and committed to the charge of the
apostolic college with Peter as its head and to their
successors. The renewed self-understanding of Chapter 3 of *On the Church* on the hierarchical structure or
the Church and in particular on the episcopate
stresses the collegial character of this ministry as it is
vested above all in the apostolic college of the Pope
and Bishops. In this way the responsibility of each
bishop and of the local church which he serves, for all
the other local churches and of all for each re-emerges
with some far reaching practical implications. The
principle of collective responsibility which is inherent
in Christianity and a distinguishing feature of Christ's
followers, God's people, applies to the special servants
of the people in a heightened fashion.

The promotion of unity of response in truth and
love to the Father for which the ordained ministry
exists in the Church is exercised through word and
sacrament. To preach Christ's word, mediate His
love through His sacraments and to preserve the
unity of the people in this truth and love, these are
the tasks of the ministry. And they are achieved
supremely in the Church's central act of self-realisa-
tion, the liturgy of the Eucharist. The Council's first
essay in self-understanding and first great charter of
renewal was the constitution, *On the Sacred Liturgy.*

At the centre of this understanding and renewal
stands the Eucharistic liturgy. The community
responds in faith to the life-giving word and is nour-
ished in charity by the sacrament of unity. It realises

for itself the central mysteries of Christ's life, death
and resurrection and is united with His complete gift
of Himself to the Father in filial love and homage. In
the Eucharist the community reaches the climax of
its relationship with Christ and so with the Father.
It becomes most fully and properly itself – the people
of God, the people in which the presence of God is
signified and realised. To do so it requires the special
ministry of the bishop or his assistant the priest to
preach the word and effect the sacrament. But it
remains primarily a community activity as sign and
realisation of the divine presence to man. It is to this
community dimension and the practical expression of
it that the renewal of the liturgy announced by
Vatican II above all addresses itself.

Has this self-understanding and the implied renewal
any connection with the problem of religious freedom?
God's presence to the world is mediated through a
people carrying on, as a people, the mission of His
Son become Man. It is itself a people freely called
by God who also respects man's freedom to answer.
One of the significant attributes of this people is their
new-found freedom as sons of God and brothers of
Christ.

Liberty is then a constant of the Christian mystery.
Christ has come to set men free. The truth which He
brings will set them free. It can only be offered to
men at all in conditions of freedom. Without the
necessary freedom, ontological, psychological and
social they cannot properly enter the free people of
God to be further mediators and witnesses of God's
presence. Unless their personal freedom to answer
God's call is respected they cannot enjoy the 'eschato-
logical' freedom of sons. Only the evidence of personal
freedom *within* the Church by which Christians may
develop as 'liberated' men and of unyielding respect
and support for personal freedom *without* it, where

men may hear and answer the free call of God, will be adequate to the Church's role as sign and realisation of the presence of supreme freedom on earth. The full exercise of freedom is in the free commitment of love. It is this love which the Father asks of men in Christ. It is this love which Christ realised in its fullness through His death and resurrection. It is this love which is made present to us in the Eucharist and which is the heart of the Christian life as it is the essence of the Christian mystery, of the God who is love. That love may flourish freedom is necessary, including the freedom of immunity from coercion in seeking and accepting the truth that contains the love and which ultimately sets men free. As a people mediating the divine presence to men, achieving its own fullness in the sacrament of Christ's love at the Eucharist and offering access to that mystery and love through free acceptance of Christ's word, the Church could not avoid recognising religious freedom as outlined in the Declaration. Anything less would not be true to the nature of the Church but rather to what Hans Küng calls its unnature, the residue of human weakness and sin which will always be part of it, as *On the Church* frankly admits. Whatever about past failure and blindness in this respect, the Church has now realised the implications of its own nature and mission to such a degree that anything less than a wholehearted endorsement of the principle of religious freedom would betray that understanding. And this was grasped however implicitly by the overwhelming majority of the fathers.

The individual documents dealing with the further details of the Church's understanding and renewal of itself such as the documents on the priesthood, religious, lay apostolate and pastoral duties of bishops do not add anything new to *On the Church, On*

Revelation and *On the Sacred Liturgy* as far as the conciliar
context of the declaration on Religious Freedom is
concerned.

The Declaration and Christian Unity

The importance of the Declaration to the 'Christian
Unity' aim of the Council scarcely needs elaboration.
One of the most sensitive points continually raised
by non-Roman Christians before and during the
Council was precisely this issue of religious liberty.
As a preliminary not just to unity but to the dialogue
demanded in search of unity, they regarded a clear-
cut affirmation of the Roman Church of the right to
religious freedom as essential. Their previous understanding of Roman Catholic theory and practice
made them fearful of the possibility of dialogue. This
is not the place to discuss the reality or otherwise of
these fears, the misunderstandings that may have
been partially responsible for them and led to the
comparisons of 'political' Roman Catholicism with
other 'totalitarian' religious or quasi-religious systems.
Neither is it the place to discuss the failures of other
Christian communities in this area in both theory and
practice.

The fact that non-Roman Christians, above all
those of them united for the promotion of Christian
unity in the World Council of Churches, regarded
such a statement as a necessary preliminary to
dialogue is the important element here. The evidence
for this attitude may be found in the reports and
statements adopted and issued by the various organs
of the World Council including its General Assembly
at Amsterdam, 1948, and New Delhi, 1961.[1] The
preoccupation with this subject and with the Roman

[1] Quoted in Carillo de Albornoz, *The Basis of Religious Freedom*,
London 1963, 157, 159.

C

Catholic attitude to it is evident also in the periodical of the World Council, The Ecumenical Review. Unless Roman Catholics recognise the right of each man to seek and accept and live religious truth freely as he discovers it, and unless they recognise the right to the legal guarantees which ensure this in society, there can be no genuine seeking the further truth of Christ together as a step towards unity in His Church. If what was commonly regarded as the Roman position – that only Roman Catholics as adherents of the one true religion really had such rights in society, which for others might only be tolerated to avoid greater evil – then dialogue, the exchange as equals which the ecumenical movement demanded, could never begin. At least in view of the recent division and confusion among Roman Catholics themselves about the matter, the Council should clearly indicate which of the conflicting views should be regarded as the truly Catholic one.

The ecumenical demands would not be satisfied by any statement whatever on religious freedom. It must, as the WCC research scholar on the matter, A. F. Carrillo de Albornoz, says in an issue of The Ecumenical Review, meet certain definite requirements in regard to the basis and range of religious freedom.[2] These requirements would bring it into line with the statement adopted by the WCC General Assembly at Amsterdam in 1948 and are outlined by Albornoz as follows (italics his):

(a) Religious Liberty must be guaranteed *as a matter of principle* and not as a matter of expediency. . . .

(b) Therefore, there are no *circumstances* under

[2] Carillo de Albornoz, *Religious Liberty and the Second Vatican Council*, in The Ecumenical Review (July 1964), 395–405.

which coercion can be justified in religious matters.

(c) The external expression of faith must be guaranteed. . . .

(d) Not only individuals should enjoy religious freedom, but there must also be *corporate religious liberty*.

(e) No citizen should suffer *discrimination or inability* on the basis of his religious beliefs or allegiance.

The object of religious freedom is further stated to be '*all the activities, commanded by religious conviction*', including 'in a particular manner the *freedom of religious witness*', which must be distinguished from proselytism, the perversion of religious witness by the use of wrong and unevangelical means.

The 'Limitations in the exercise of religious liberty' must be stated carefully so:

(a) that any limitation in the exercise of religious liberty should be expressly regulated by law and by no means left to the discretionary power of the civil authorities or of the police;

(b) that any limitation should always be based on the grounds of the temporal common good of the civil society;

(c) that it must be made without any discrimination between citizens or between the different religions.

As a basis for limitation of religious freedom, common good should, he says, be limited 'to the civil common good of the temporal society', but 'the civil common good' should not be made the basis for the right itself.

He goes on to list some corollaries to the principle of religious freedom governing Church-State rela-

tionship which he would like to see 'clearly proclaimed':

    (a) The Church in her spiritual commission does
        not depend on the civil society.
    (b) Therefore the state must limit itself to the
        temporal order. . . .
    (c) As a consequence, the welfare which the state
        has the right and duty to protect, is exclusively
        the temporal common good. . . .
    (d) Therefore the state by limiting in some cases
        the exercise of religious activities cannot do so
        with discrimination between different religions.

The formulation of the Council's approach to
unity in the *Decree on Ecumenism* gives some indica-
tions from within the Church of the need for a statement affirming religious freedom and the lines it
should take.

The decree begins by stating that 'the restoration
of unity among all Christians is one of the principal
concerns of the Second Vatican Council'. It recognises the movement for unity among our separated
brethren as 'fostered by the grace of the Holy Spirit'.
The Roman Church while conscious of its substantial
continuity with the original community of Peter and
the Twelve founded by Christ, gladly acknowledges
'That all who have been justified by faith in baptism
are incorporated into Christ; they therefore have a
right to be called Christians, and with good reason
are accepted as brothers by the children of the
Catholic Church'.

It is not a question however of accepting individuals.
These individuals live in 'communities' or 'Churches'
which contain 'some, even very many of the most
significant elements which together go to build up and
give life to the Church itself . . .; the written word

of God; the life of grace; faith, hope and charity, with the other interior gifts of the Holy Spirit, as well as visible elements'. These communities have much of the Christian liturgy which in various degrees 'can truly engender a life of grace, and one must say, can aptly give access to the communion of salvation'. So these separated churches are used by the Spirit of Christ and have their own 'significance and importance in the mystery of salvation'.

The Council commits the whole Church to this work of promoting unity and proclaims it the concern of all, clergy and laity alike. The programme which they must follow is spiritual, intellectual and social. A necessary part of the spiritual programme is prayer together, private and in particular circumstances public, so that they may at once manifest the limited unity that exists between them and humbly ask the Father for growth in this unity. The study involves an effort to understand the other more fully and explain oneself more effectively. Particularly important are the meetings of competent experts from the different churches, coming together as equals and 'searching together into the divine mysteries'. Finally their unity in truth and love will be promoted by common enterprises in the service of man in all his various social and individual needs. In this way they will bear particular witness to their common adhesion to Christ the servant of all and remove much of the scandal of division.

Thus, in the light of the explicit demands of other Christians for a statement on religious liberty as a necessary condition for fruitful ecumenical dialogue and in the light of the attitude of the Council to the ecumenical movement as a work of the Holy Spirit, to other Christians as genuine brothers in Christ and to their churches as instruments of salvation as well as of the programme of action laid down in Chapter 2

of *On Ecumenism* a statement on religious freedom was
clearly demanded. How would one reconcile, for
instance, the common worship of Pope Paul with the
observers or the Decree's provisions for common
worship between Catholics and other Christians with
the view that public worship of these Christians could
only be tolerated by the state to avoid a greater evil?

It seems safe to say that the Council's Declaration
satisfies the main requirements of separated Christians. Religious freedom is recognised as a matter of
principle to exclude all coercion and includes the
public social domain as well as the private and
individual. The only limitations are those imposed for
the sake of that section of 'the civil common good of
the temporal society' called 'public order'. It further
recognises the independence of the Church and the
limitations of the State's competence to the temporal
order along the general lines suggested by de Albornoz.
He himself describes it as 'a great document, possibly
at least in ecumenical perspective, the greatest that
has emerged from the long debates of the Second
Vatican Council'. It is no less satisfactory in providing the general framework within which the programme of *De Ecumenismo* and the unity intentions of
the Council itself may be implemented.

Relations with Non-Christians

In the context of the world at large, the ecumenical
dimensions of the Declaration might be described as
domestic, concerned with the internal relations of a
diminishing minority. The scope of the Council's
programme and the intentions of this Declaration
were however much wider, that is ecumenical in its
original sense of reaching out to all men of the
inhabited earth. Religious freedom affects all men,

even men who are irreligious or anti-religions. The Christian's attitude to men of all religions and none, as expressed in the documents, *Declaration on the Relation of the Church to Non-Christian Religions* and the *Pastoral Constitution on the Church in the Modern World*, presupposes, illuminates and harmonises with the Declaration on Religious Freedom. Without such a clear-cut statement on religious freedom these documents would lack in clarity and impact.

The *Declaration on Non-Christian Religions* recognises their value in general and asserts that 'the Catholic Church rejects nothing that is true and holy in these religions'. Positive elements in the beliefs and moral codes of the Hindus, Buddhists and Moslems are briefly listed with approval, with the intention of promoting good relations between themselves and Christians. The Jews receive more extended treatment for obvious reasons and 'in her rejection of every persecution against any man the Church mindful of the patrimony she shares with the Jews and moved not by political reasons but by the Gospel's spiritual love, decries hatred, persecutions, displays of anti-semitism directed against Jews at any time and by anyone'.

The declaration concludes with a strong statement condemning 'any discrimination against men or harassment of them because of their race, colour, condition in life, or religion'. To be able to address God as Father, Christians must treat all men as brothers and rule out all such discrimination.

Respect for non-Christian religions, expressed here, desires to live in harmony with them and the severe condemnations of discrimination or persecution on religious grounds among others make this Declaration a useful complement to that on Religious Freedom. One would be incomplete without the other.

Dialogue with the World

But not all people are religious. And the point of the
Declaration was that nobody may be coerced to be.
A. F. Carrillo de Albornoz in The Ecumenical
Review may be unfair in his qualified criticism of it
in regard to the guarantees of freedom for non-
believers or atheists. He says: 'We cannot avoid the
impression that the general context and spirit of the
whole Declaration seems to be rather contrary to
this "Atheistic freedom".'[3] The Declaration certainly does not seem so to me and if it is taken in con-
junction with the document on *The Church in the
Modern World* there can be no doubt of the Council's
awareness of the existence and rights of these people.

The very long and occasionally rambling statement
of the Church's relationship with the modern world
underlines a number of matters which have a bearing
on the religious freedom issue in addition to the
specific treatment of atheists. The Church sees itself
as fulfilling the role of Christ in the service of mankind by fostering above all 'the brotherhood of all
men which corresponds to this destiny of theirs'(§3).
So it addresses itself to all mankind inspired by no
earthly ambition and seeking but a solitary goal: 'to
carry forward the work of Christ under the lead of the
befriending Spirit. And Christ entered this world
to give witness to the truth, to rescue and not to sit
in judgement, to serve and not to be served' (§3).

This service of mankind the Church discharges by
preserving and promoting the true dignity of man.
This dignity involves seeking truth and goodness in
freedom. The contemporary concern for freedom is
also the Church's in its desire to proclaim and protect
the rights of man. In service of mankind, believers

[3] Carillo de Albornoz, *The Declaration on Religious Liberty*, The
Ecumenical Review (January 1966).

and unbelievers should co-operate fully through various enterprises. Such freedom and co-operation would be unthinkable apart from complete immunity from coercion in religious matters, applied to atheists as well as believers.

In preserving the dignity and promoting the unity of mankind, the Council document devotes a special section to the 'setting up an International Community' and it gives special commendation to 'already existing international regional organisations'. Such organisations can only develop as the document is well aware where basic human rights including the right to religious freedom are guaranteed. The inclusion of such a right in the Declaration of the United Nations Organisation (Article 18) and in the European Convention of Human Rights (Article 9) in terms very akin to the Council's Declaration shows the necessity for such a Declaration in the context of the Church's approach to the modern world. The document in a number of places refers to religious freedom as a necessary consequence of human dignity and necessary condition of human development. And it deals in some detail with the problem of atheism (§19).

It is admitted that 'many of our contemporaries have never recognised this intimate and vital link with God, or have explicitly rejected it'. Atheism may be of different kinds and varying degrees of responsibility. And believers themselves must often bear responsibility for the unbelief in the world. The remedy however is not any coercion or conditioning but 'a proper presentation of the Church's teaching as well as the integral life of the Church and her members. What does most reveal God's presence, however, is the brotherly charity of the faithful . . .' (§21).

Religious freedom is guaranteed to atheists. Indeed 'the Church protests against the distinction which some State authorities make between believers and unbelievers, with prejudice to the fundamental rights of the human person' (§21).

Guarantee of their freedom is also implied in the co-operation and dialogue with atheists which the Church, in spite of its rejection of atheism in itself, sees as right and necessary for the service of mankind. 'While rejecting atheism, root and branch, the Church sincerely professes that all men, believers and unbelievers, ought to work for the rightful betterment of this world in which all alive live; such an ideal cannot be realised, however, apart from sincere and prudent dialogue' (§21).

The relationship so strikingly achieved by Pope John with all men of good will and so effectively expressed in his encyclical *Peace on Earth* is further developed in this pastoral constitution. The emphasis on the Church's service of man and his rights demands and implies full recognition of religious freedom. And a comparison of the two documents, *The Church in the World* and *Religious Freedom*, prevents any possible misunderstanding in regard to atheists or unbelievers.

With the deeper understanding of the Church's nature and so of its relations with other Christians and all mankind, which the major conciliar documents present, the recognition of religious freedom harmonises perfectly. Indeed the Declaration expresses in a definite form a constant theme of these documents – man's freedom as an essential consequence of the dignity he enjoys as created in the image of God and called to sonship of God. In very many ways the Council was concerned with freedom, freedom of and freedom for man and the Christian. The Declaration marks a signal achievement in this cause of human and Christian freedom and it allows the Church to be more truly herself in her relationship with all men, Christian, non-Christian and irreligious. As a pledge of the Church's genuine commitment to men's loving service and as a constant reminder of the Church's true reality and mission, the Declaration on Religious Freedom may prove to be as important as its ardent supporters (and opponents) believed and as the numerous crises and constant publicity suggested.

5. Religious Freedom and the State[1]

The problem of religious freedom and the State is one of the most explosive points at issue between Roman Catholics and other Christians. This was forcibly brought to our notice by the controversies surrounding the American presidential election. But even a cursory glance at current Protestant literature reveals how deeply entrenched is the belief that Roman Catholicism, with its absolutist claims, is the enemy of religious freedom and wishes to abolish it, wherever it is strong enough to do so.

That is the position of extremists like Paul Blanshard. The titles of his allegedly scientific studies of the problem created by the Church's claims are sufficiently revealing: *The Irish and Catholic Power;*[2] *American Freedom and Catholic Power;*[3] *Communism, Democracy and Catholic Power.*[4]

The temptation to dismiss Blanshard and his friends in POAU (Protestants and Other Americans United for Separation of Church and State) as too fanatical, and indeed dishonest, to be worthy of refutation is very strong. Yet they give expression,

---

[1] First published in *Christian Unity*, Maynooth, 1962.
[2] Boston 1953.   [3] Boston 1953 (First ed. 1949).
[4] Boston 1952.

however unfairly, to a widespread conviction amongst even charitable and well-informed non-Catholics. As evidence of this we may cite the favourable notices given to books such as Blanshard's in the official publication of the World Council of Churches, The Ecumenical Review.[5]

A survey of Protestant writers, free from any suggestion of Blanshard's hysteria, reveals the strength of this belief in the opposition of Catholicism to religious freedom. In doctrine and in practice, where they are strong enough, Roman Catholics reject the freedom of the individual to profess and propagate any religion other than their own. Even such prominent and far from sectarian theologians as Karl Barth can be quoted as using the quite frequent comparisons of Catholicism and Communism, of Rome and Moscow in relation to the freedom of the individual.[6] Quite sympathetic studies of Roman Catholicism aimed at promoting better relations between the Christian bodies interpret the Catholic attitude to religious freedom in the same fashion.

A good example of such a study is Jaroslav Pelikan's *The Riddle of Roman Catholicism*, London 1960. On our problem he writes:

> Political theorists of the Roman communion have quite candidly admitted that the ideal of 'a Catholic Church in a Catholic State' implies recognition by the State of the Church's prior rights and privileges and a refusal to grant similar rights and privileges to other religious bodies. When it is

[5] Cf. review of Blanshard's *American Freedom and Catholic Power* by Henry Smith Leiper in The Ecumenical Review, 2 (1950), no. 2, 217 and review of James Hastings Nichols, *Democracy and the Churches*, Philadelphia 1951, by the same reviewer, *E. R.*, 3 (1951), no. 4, 428. Smith Leiper is a former Associate General Secretary of the World Council of Churches.

[6] J. S. Whale, *The Protestant Tradition*, London 1960, 236.

in a controlling majority, the Church refuses to put error on the same level as truth; it is therefore committed to intolerance. Meanwhile it demands a tolerance for itself which in principle it would refuse to others.[7]

There can be no ignoring then the real difficulty which religious freedom presents for those seriously concerned about Christian unity. The World Council in its various discussions and publications has displayed great interest in it. Some reference to it appears in most issues of The Ecumenical Review. A special Research Associate for Religious Liberty, Dr A. F. Carrillo de Albornoz, appointed by the Council, wrote a series of articles in the review which were afterwards published as a booklet with the title *Roman Catholicism and Religious Liberty*.[8] This booklet may well prove to be the most important contribution from outside the Church towards solving the difficulties about religious freedom in the ecumenical dialogue between Catholics and Protestants.

There has been no lack of Catholic interest either. A vast literature by Catholic theologians on this topic has appeared in the last decade. And the setting of this study has been to a great extent ecumenical – intended to clarify and justify the Catholic position for other Christians.

Neither the clarification nor the justification have been entirely successful. The Protestant conviction that our position is unjustifiable we have seen to be still very widespread. And the clarification, while it is growing, is far from complete. Perhaps it would be better to say that the clarification has grown in two quite different if not contradictory directions. There

[7] Op. cit., 100.
[8] Carillo de Albornoz, *Roman Catholicism and Religious Liberty*, Geneva 1959.

is undoubtedly a great deal of truth in the comment of American Protestant theologian John C. Bennett summarising the situation in 1958:

> A . . . fact about Roman Catholicism that needs to be understood by Protestants is that the Catholic Church is divided from top to bottom in this country and abroad in regard to religious liberty.[9]

The existence of some such division on the theory if not the practice of religious freedom is undeniable. So is the consequent weakness of our position in discussing the matter with other Christians. Without a single agreed position of our own, we find it very difficult to define our disagreements with others and still more difficult to deal effectively with the blatantly hostile campaign of a man like Blanshard. The unfavourable brand image of the Church, so widespread in the post-Christian world, is due in great measure to the belief that the Church is intolerant and dictatorial. For this reason, Cardinal Lercaro, echoing many Catholic voices throughout the world, describes the development of the correct theology of tolerance or religious freedom as one of the most urgent tasks facing theologians to-day.[10]

With this development still in progress, the Church's teaching cannot be presented in any final or definitive form. Neither is it possible to proceed in the normal theological way from authoritative and definitive statements by the magisterium to explanation and proof. Statements from the magisterium, particularly from the Popes, we have in plenty. These statements are obviously of first importance in studying the problem. Yet there is so much dispute about their

[9] John C. Bennett, *Christians and the State*, New York 1958.
[10] Cardinal Lercaro, *Tolleranza e intolleranza religiosa*, Sacra Doctrina, 3 (1958), no. 10, 144.

correct interpretation that it would be unprofitable, indeed impossible, within the confines of this paper to attempt to base the doctrine of religious freedom directly on an analysis of the papal teaching. We go instead to the sources behind the papal teaching, revelation and reason, and try to construct the general outlines of a theology of religious freedom on these foundations. In this construction, account must be taken, at least implicitly, of the papal directives, not however by an assembly of isolated sentences and passages taken out of context, but by a deeper understanding of the Pope's pronouncements delivered in a definite historical situation and frequently aimed at very definite historical errors.

False Solutions

Before presenting the true theological foundations of tolerance, we must discuss certain false foundations on which religious freedom is frequently based.

To deny the existence of any objective order of truth, or at least to deny the possibility of ever certainly knowing it, leads immediately to religious indifferentism. One religion becomes as good or as bad, as true or as false as another. There could be no question then of any religion enjoying special rights or privileges, and no reason to restrict anybody's religious beliefs and practices. Such scepticism seems the easy way to justifying religious freedom and its development was closely associated with these errors.

For the Catholic Church such an approach is impossible. She upholds the existence of a divinely established objective order of truth, which man can certainly know. She further claims to have exclusive possession of this divine truth and denies that there is any essential error in her presentation of it. Indeed every religion which believes in God and in a revelation must stand by certain truths as necessary and objective, if it is to mean anything. 'We cannot admit', says Swiss Protestant theologian David Lersch, 'that two contradictory statements in the moral or religious order are equally valid'.[11]

It was in this spirit that the Protestants over four centuries campaigned against the errors of Catholics as well as against those of other Protestant bodies. Protestant certainty of the objective truth of Christianity is still very alive. The certainty of the individual possession and understanding of it has been somewhat shaken by the new consciousness of the serious divisions amongst Christians, even amongst Protestants, and by the growing desire to heal these. It may have been these reasons that moved Reinhold Niebuhr to declare that a certain element of scepticism about one's own grasp of the truth is necessary for tolerance.[12]

The Catholic Church remains unshaken in its consciousness of its certain possession of the truth. On this there can be no compromise. She can never admit that one religion is as good or as true as another. Such a basis for tolerance is unacceptable to her.

This attitude of the Church to the truth and its necessity is sometimes described as dogmatic intolerance.[13] The expression is unfortunate, because it may be so easily misleading, and is much better avoided.

A more subtle but equally false approach to this

[11] *Das Problem der Toleranz in theologischer Sicht*, Zurich 1948, 10.
[12] Quoted in Niels H. Soe, *The Theological Basis of Religious Liberty*, The Ecumenical Review, 11 (1958), no. 1, 38.
[13] Cf. Pribilla, *Dogmatische Intoleranz und bürgerliche Toleranz*, Stimmen der Zeit, 144 (1949), no. 7, 27 ff.

problem is to maintain that religion is each man's private affair. It has therefore no relevance for the State or public life. But public and political activity has, as the Christian knows, a moral and therefore religious aspect. Far from being a solution of tolerance such a solution, by ignoring the conscientious demands of citizens who recognise the moral aspect of political activity, would effectively destroy religious freedom. It was this form of solution, based ultimately on a denial of religious truth, which was attempted in the Third Republic in France, of which it was said that it ignored the Church, except when it wished to persecute her.

The Thesis-Hypothesis Approach

These false approaches have been frequently and vigorously rejected by the Catholic Church. Their development, however, had some unfortunate influences on the Catholic attitude to religious freedom, from which it has not as yet entirely recovered. In the excitement which accompanied the rejection of these errors, the true notion of this freedom was obscured. And the predominant form of Catholic answer in terms of thesis and hypothesis which emerged towards the end of the nineteenth century has proved unsatisfactory, although it is still with us. Today, however, it is much less widely accepted, at least in its original form.

This solution of the problem[14] denies in principle or *in thesi* the right of those in religious error to profess and propagate those errors publicly in the State. *In hypothesi*, however, or in the concrete situation where repression of these errors is impossible or would do

[14] A typical presentation of this solution may be found in Sutillo-Regatillo, *Compendium Juris Publici Ecclesiastici*, Santander 1958.

more harm than good, the State may permit such public profession. Religious freedom is permitted where it cannot be avoided. And the arguments adduced to support this position generally reduce to variations on the assertion 'error has no rights' or 'false religions may not be given equal status with the true'.

The thesis or the ideal situation, as it is sometimes described, is the so-called Catholic State in which the Catholic Church is recognised as the one true Church and given certain juridical privileges, while the public profession and propagation of other religions is not legally permitted. The State, it is argued, has as God's creature parallel obligations to that of the individual to recognise effectively the true religion, i.e. the Catholic Church and so to protect her from the dangers of invading heretics. Reason and revelation demand as much, as the series of papal texts collected from Gregory XVI, Pius XI and Leo XIII bears witness. In practice, however, where Catholics are not the ruling authority or are not sufficiently powerful, other religions may be tolerated.

It is important to emphasise that the defenders of this view reject any suggestion that anybody may be forced to become a Catholic. They simply deny the citizen's right to profess any other religion publicly in the Catholic State. And of course only in very exceptional cases will the denial in principle take legal effect in practice.

To do complete justice to this approach would demand much more extensive treatment than is possible here. It is still widely defended in the Church. Indeed it is the only Catholic approach of which most Protestants and others show any awareness. And it has drawn their most bitter criticism. For them it may be summed up in the sentence falsely attributed to the nineteenth-century controversialist, Louis Veullot: 'When we are a minority, we demand freedom because that is your (i.e. non-Catholic) principle; when we are a majority we deny it to you, because that is our principle.'

Towards a Satisfactory Solution

It is not, of course, because it is so unacceptable to Protestants that I reject this approach here as unsatisfactory, but because it is so unacceptable to Catholics. With its suggestion of expediency and sharp practice, it offends our Catholic instinct of charity, of doing to others as we would have them to do us. And on examination the arguments for it prove quite unconvincing. The correct theology of religious freedom which is now receiving increased study and recognition from Catholic theologians all over the world[15] is in no way based on the errors of indifferentism or on the irrelevance of religion to public life. And it has none of the doctrinal or strategic disadvantages of the thesis-hypothesis approach. It has a firm foundation in the dignity of man as a spiritual being and adopted son of God, in the nature and limitations of the State's competence, in the freedom of the act of faith and in the common good of Church and State.

The Philosophical Basis

In creating man, God made him in His own image by giving him the spiritual faculties of intellect and

[15] The booklet by Dr. Carillo de Albornoz is an excellent survey of the theological literature which defends this view up to 1959. Amongst the more important works are: *Tolérance et communauté humaine*, Symposium, Paris 1952; Maritain, *Man and the State*, London 1954; Hartmann, *Toleranz und Christlicher Glaube*, Frankfurt am M. 1955 and the articles of Father Courtney Murray, S.J., which appeared in *Theological Studies* in the 'fifties.

will, the powers to know and love, to act freely and deliberately. At the same time He invited man to share His own divine knowledge and love by faith and charity in this life and by the union of the Beatific Vision in the next. In making this offer God scrupulously respected man's personal freedom. And when man used that freedom to reject the invitation, God renewed it even to the extent of sending His own Son to lay down His life for man and so draw him back to the ultimate goal of personal union with his eternal Father. Man's response to the invitation manifested in Christ and His Church is his only road to perfection and happiness. And he must answer it as a man, knowingly and freely. The judgement by which man decides what God wants of him in a particular situation we call conscience. In following his conscience then, in seeking to live in accordance with the truth as he knows it, man is fulfilling God's will.

Because this is his duty, it is also man's right. No human authority may interfere to compel a man to act contrary to his conscience, to God's will as he knows it. 'For we ought to obey God rather than men'.[16] True freedom of conscience then is not any autonomy of the individual as creator of his own truths and values, but the right of each man to seek the truth about himself, his destiny and his God, and to act in accordance with it. Whatever his destiny or perfection, man must seek it knowingly and freely. His nature demands as much. But his nature also demands that he seek that destiny in society, for he is not only an intelligent free being but also a social one. His perfection he can achieve only in society. And that society which is natural and necessary for him, when it is organised by law to protect his rights as a free being as well as to provide for the other needs of his nature, we call the State.

[16] Acts 5:29.

The State exists then to serve man, to promote by law, which is the State's proper mode of activity, the welfare of its citizens. It can do this only if it respects man's dignity as a person with his personal gifts of intelligence and free will. And it must above all respect and protect man's right to seek his final perfection or destiny, knowingly and freely. This destiny is not immediately and infallibly known to each man. But the State may not impose any particular solution to this problem, even the correct one, on its citizens. And it must protect man's freedom of conscience, even when that conscience is in error.

But yet, as a necessary society for the promotion of man's perfection, the State must defend its own existence and provide a certain minimum of peace and order and try to compose the basic rights of all the citizens. Man's right to act in accordance with the truth as he sees it is not unlimited then. Where such activity threatens the very basis of society, as with the conscientious anarchist, the State may and should forbid it. Similarly, activity which interferes with the just rights to life, property, good name of other citizens or which disturbs the public order of the society will be forbidden by the State, which has the duty of upholding the general welfare even against the conscientious activities of particular citizens. There are some activities such as ritual murder which no State may tolerate.

Based on man's nature and aimed at his perfection, the State may not frustrate that nature by imposing anything contrary to it, anything which violates the natural law. Indeed since the observance of the natural law is necessary for human perfection, the State should endeavour to promote it publicly. And public violations of it, as they are opposed to that public welfare which is the State's precise care, should normally be outlawed.

But a State is not merely a natural and necessary society. It is also an actual and historical one, composed of particular people with their own individual beliefs and practices which may fall short of the requirements of the natural law. The State must take account of these beliefs and practices in its laws, and for the sake of a greater good, the peace and order of society, as well as the protection of individual consciences, sometimes permit public departures from natural law. The classic instance of this is the legalised permission of prostitution in certain countries – an example also used by Saint Augustine. Instead of outlawing a particular practice, the State will in these circumstances encourage the educational and religious forces in society to improve the general moral standard and gradually render such legal tolerance unnecessary.

This natural morality which the State must uphold as part of the common good, and which is ideally identical with the natural law, but in reality frequently less than that, we call public morality. The State has a duty to defend public morality as well as public order against even the conscientious activities of its citizens. Freedom of conscience, in so far as that concerns public activity, must submit to the limitations of public order and public morality. Within these limits each citizen should enjoy the protection of the law in living in accordance with his conscience.

The Theological Argument

This defence of freedom of conscience, of man's freedom to seek the truth about his destiny and to live according to that truth as he knows it, has abstracted from the more exact determination of that destiny, which we mentioned at the beginning and which is known from the Christian Revelation. We have been concerned rather with the philosophical notions of man as a free, intelligent being and the State as a necessary society based on man's nature. And the conclusions which we have drawn about freedom of conscience receive a new depth and force when they are examined in the light of the supernatural character of man's destiny and of the supernatural means necessary to attain it. Here the argument becomes more precisely theological and the freedom more precisely religious.

The act of faith which is the *initium* and *radix* of the life of grace to which God calls all men is essentially free. This freedom is exercised in the first instance by God Himself, in calling a person to the true faith. The mystery of God's free vocation must be kept in mind in considering State interference with a man's religious beliefs, where the State arrogates to itself this divine right.

The act of faith is also the free assent of the human person to a set of truths. These truths are not self-evident, and the evidence presented is evidence of credibility. Assent still depends on the free movement of the will. Any state imposition of religious belief would be a negation of this freedom and an absurdity. Even to restrict by law the rights of citizens simply because they do not accept a particular religious faith seems to infringe the necessary human freedom of the act of faith and to show a grave misunderstanding of the workings of God. Where people are penalised by the civil authority for their religious beliefs, either directly by State fines or imprisonment or indirectly by unfair taxation, the unfair use of public moneys in such a matter as education or the virtual closing of particular careers, there is unwarranted interference with the freedom of the act of faith and a serious temptation to insincerity, which would make the faith meaningless.

The incompetence of the State in all these matters

stands fully revealed when we consider that Christ instituted a special society with its own divine authority to cater for man's religious needs. The foundation of the Church was a revolutionary step in this matter, because man is now subject to two distinct human authorities as two distinct societies. As a citizen with his natural needs and his desire for natural development and perfection, he remains a member of the State and subject to its authority. But in seeking his final destiny or perfection, which is supernatural, he belongs to a new society and is subject to a new authority. The relationship of man to God which is generally described in man's religion has now become the exclusive concern of the Church.

It is not the business of the State then, as emphasised by Leo XIII, to save souls, to bring people to heaven, to accept responsibility and authority for the religious life of the citizens. The State may not ignore or be indifferent to religion. Religion is necessary for man and for his ultimate perfection. The State's concern is man's perfection, not his supernatural, ultimate perfection, but the natural, immediate perfection of his nature which each man desires and seeks and which should be the basis of his supernatural life and perfection. The State on the pretext of promoting this natural perfection may not interfere with man's pursuit of his higher destiny or with the freedom of the Church, who is the custodian of the true religion and the divinely-authorised guide for each man. The freedom of the Church, the freedom of each man to answer Christ's call to the new life, and to do that in the Church as soon as he recognises her divine mission – these freedoms are superior to all State authority. And the fact that an individual errs in his conception of Christ's call and of religious belief does not give the State any new competence over him or any right to correct him.

By religious freedom we mean, then, not that each man is morally free before God to choose any or no religion, but that he may not be hindered by the State in seeking to know the truth about himself and God and in seeking to live according to this truth, as he knows it. The philosophical basis for this freedom is deepened by considering the supernatural character of man's final destiny in the present order, God's freedom in calling him to that destiny, man's freedom in responding to it and by the establishment of a society and authority independent of the State with full responsibility for man's supernatural or religious life.

The Range of Religious Freedom

Freedom of religion naturally implies freedom of external profession and freedom of propagation. Freedom of belief without freedom of external and public profession would be less than human, and a man who believes that he has the true religion is morally driven to propagate it.

Freedom of religion, freedom to believe, profess and propagate that religion which one regards as true independently of the State authority is a basic human right. But, as with other human rights, it cannot in society be unlimited. The limitations which are imposed by the very nature of civil society, that is, ultimately, by the nature of man, the philosophical discussion of man and the State has shown to be public order and public morality. Nothing appears in the later theological approach which would change this.

Public order remains a first requirement in the State. Modes of profession or propagation of religion which are deliberately provocative and calculated to cause breaches of the peace may and should be restricted by the civil authorities. When is such provocation caused? Which modes of propagation are likely to lead to breaches of the peace? These are difficult questions, calling for very delicate judgement in the actual circumstances of the particular State. The attempt of a misguided Catholic preacher to address Northern Protestants from the steps of an Orange Hall on the failings of Luther and Calvin would certainly be such. Such a clear-cut example seldom occurs, although it would seem that some of the activities of the North American Protestant missionaries in South America have been provocative in the past.

This anxiety for the public peace or the security of the State was at the root of much of the medieval and Reformation persecution of heretics and non-conformers by Catholic and Protestant princes. Political unity seemed impossible without religious unity. The loyal citizen must *eo ipso* be a Christian in medieval Christendom, a Catholic in sixteenth-century France, an Anglican in Tudor England. Membership of any religion other than the prince's (*cuius regio, eius religio*) was sedition and treated as such. And it seems certain that much of Spain's problem to-day is related to the acceptance of the connexion between religious and political unity.

In most western countries, however, people no longer regard this connection as inevitable. And religious unity is not now regarded as part of the State's common good. The development in the State's consciousness of its natural function and of its complete distinction from the supernatural society, the Church, proved a necessary forerunner to the clarification of religious freedom.

The second limitation to religious freedom in the State, the preservation of public morality, calls for

more careful and lengthier consideration. To say that
the problem of religious freedom today reduces to
the problem of public morality is to exaggerate, but
in some States only to a slight degree.

Religion connotes not merely a set of beliefs, but
also a way of life, based on these beliefs. As a way of
life, it will naturally impinge on that public morality
which the State must protect as part of the common
good of its citizens and which it must promote as an
aid in their natural development. Public morality we
have seen to be ideally identical with the natural law,
but actually frequently less than that. In seeking to
promote the natural welfare of its citizens the State
must take account of their actual moral beliefs and
practices, and so sometimes refrain from outlawing
public breaches of natural law morality for the sake
of such higher goods as the protection of the individual
conscience and the harmony and security of the
State. This legal permission of immoral practices,
such as for example prostitution, may be properly
called tolerance, as the State permits something which
absolutely speaking it could forbid. It must be distinguished from religious freedom strictly understood,
which is based on the State's incompetence in the
religious field. But where the members of a religious
group advocate activities which are contrary to
public morality, the State is within its competence in
forbidding these. The classic example of this is the
United States prohibition of polygamy advocated by
the Mormons, as opposed to the morality generally
accepted in the United States or the public morality
there. Although the State can tolerate practices contrary to the natural law, whether founded on religious
belief or not, for the sake of a higher good, it can and
should outlaw such practices, even if they are demanded in the name of religion, where they are
opposed to the public morality generally accepted in

the State. Religious freedom is limited not merely by the demands of public order in the narrower sense of peace or order, but also by those of public morality.

In principle this presents no particular difficulty. In practice the task of estimating the level of public morality, of determining how far the State may permit or should forbid public violations of the natural law, especially those closely associated with religious belief, becomes infinitely delicate and complex. It calls for co-operation and the highest prudence amongst religious and political leaders. And in an increasing number of countries it is the central problem of religious freedom. In countries where religious pluralism is accepted as one of the facts of life, freedom of religious belief, profession and propagation are in themselves not an issue. But the great variety of belief and practice on such complicated issues as divorce, contraception, abortion, homosexuality and so on, and the variety of laws to which these have given rise cause innumerable delicate problems of conscience, of prudence and of patience.

The attitude that such practices are contrary to the natural law and that therefore they should be automatically outlawed is not adequate, as Catholic theologians have long recognised. The natural law, as we understand it, is not accepted in its entirety by people outside the Church. Indeed our exposition of it depends on the fuller knowledge of revelation and the infallible guidance of the Church. And, as Saint Thomas pointed out, a civil prohibition must be adapted to the conditions of the community if it is to be effective. Where the moral basis of a particular prohibition is widely rejected or where the established practice of the community would render it impossible to enforce, civil prohibition will do more harm than good and some legal control of the evil may be adopted as the best solution in the circumstances.

The difficulty of combining a genuine interest in the promotion of good morals, respect for the conscientious beliefs of the citizens and a degree of realism (which is not the same as pessimism) about the effectiveness of law presents the statesman with many problems. Obviously he may not yield to every voice raised in the cause of greater laxity. Neither can he ignore the conscientious demands of a large group of citizens. Where a particular legal tolerance is operating with some effective control of the evil, he will be slow to withdraw that. Where the tolerance is demanded by the few and the prohibition is clearly preventing a social evil and in accord with the wishes of the majority, he will not yield. His criterion, however, may never be the simple counting of heads, but the common good, where that includes the promotion of good morals and the protection of the weak, such as children, as well as the rights of conscience and civil order. In enabling the statesmen and politicians to arrive at a proper evaluation of the common good in this matter and so the demands of public morality, Catholics should make their views known clearly and honestly both about the morality of the practice under discussion and the possibility of permitting or outlawing it By such rational and honest discussion the best solution in the circumstances will be obtained.

Within the limits then of public order and public morality, the State should guarantee every citizen freedom to profess, practise and propagate his religion. The philosophical and theological arguments on which this claim is based are confirmed by a consideration of the common good of the State and of that of the Church, and of the relations between them.

If the State be pluralist in religion – and most modern States are – any discrimination on the grounds of religious belief would inevitably harm the peaceful co-operation of all the citizens for the common good, and would reduce the contribution of the particular 'restricted' group to the common good, where it did not lead to civil strife. Even a State exclusively of one religion would in the complex international situation of today suffer in its relations with States whose religion or religions it did not tolerate. Modern States are so economically and militarily interdependent that the resultant damage could be great.

The Church suffers in its mission also from any intolerance performed in its name. The association of Rome and Moscow, Catholicism and Communism, already noted, springs from real or alleged intolerance in the past as well as a particular understanding of Catholic doctrine in the matter. All this may be attributed to bad faith or misinformation or an exaggerated notion of the rights of the individual, but it is a distinct handicap to the Church in furthering her mission of salvation. The development and teaching of the correct doctrine on religious freedom seem the only way to remove this handicap.

The strategic or political advantages of the doctrine of religious freedom as outlined seem obvious, but of course its justification lies in a correct understanding of man, the Church and the State. And the arguments advanced against it, by some Catholic writers, may be effective in demolishing a false religious freedom based on indifferentism. They do not impinge on this position.

'Error has no rights' is in itself a meaningless statement except in so far as it may be understood as error is wrong. Only persons can have rights. And the possible paraphrases 'persons in error have no rights' or 'persons in error have not the same rights as those in truth' help but little. Persons have rights in relation to other persons and authorities. And the right of religious freedom does not mean any right against God to adopt any religion or none, but the right in the face of the civil authority to seek to know and serve God in accordance with one's conscience, even if that conscience be in error.

The State's protection of religious freedom in this sense does not equiparate truth and falsehood. It does not pronounce on the truth and falsehood of the religions at all, because the State is not competent to do so. And the State does not grant the right of religious freedom, it recognises and protects this God-given right in the individual citizen.

The argument from the Catholic State thesis and the State's duty to recognise and protect the Church to the necessary repression of other religions, even if it were cogent,[17] must finally shatter on its misconception of the basic principles governing Church-State relations. The harmony and co-operation which should exist between these two distinct and independent societies will vary in form and legal expression from age to age and from State to State. The Catholic State was one historical form or expression of this harmony, which is not necessarily valid or suitable in our own day and which must always take account of the right of the individual to seek his destiny as outlined in this paper.

The papal documents are not conclusive for either side. The claims made by some of the thesis-hypothesis school for particular texts from the nineteenth-century Popes never take sufficient account of the historical situation in which they were issued or of

---

[17] In an article in Periodica, 48 (1959), 3-4, 298 ff., *Obligationis Status veram religionem profitendi praemissae et limites*, R. Bortolotti denies that you can deduce the State's obligation to repress heresy from its obligation to profess the true religion. He deduces it rather from the State's obligation to defend the true religion against the propagation of heresy, etc.

the particular errors which they were combating – in some cases, for example, freedom from religion rather than freedom of religion. The later statements of Leo XIII,[18] those of Pius XI[19] in his struggles against the new totalitarianisms, Fascism, Nazism and Communism, and those of Pius XII dealing with the values of democracy[20] as well as with the specific problem of tolerance,[21] provide more positive support for the doctrine of religious freedom as expounded here. But the magisterium has not finally clarified and settled the issue. A good deal of hard thinking and vigorous writing must still be done before a satisfactory theology of religious freedom will be fully developed and accepted.

Conclusion

The aim of this paper has been to introduce and to attempt to solve the problem of religious freedom and the State as a problem for ecumenism. It has been a serious source of friction between Catholics and Protestants as well as amongst Catholics themselves. It is urgently required that Catholics find a solution to their own differences and then try to put that solution as clearly as possible to other Christians.

That solution, I suggest, is the full protection by the State of freedom of religion – including profession, practice and propagation within the bounds of public order and public morality. This seems to be most in

[18] In the encyclical *Libertas* of Leo XIII, for instance, ASS 20 (1887–88), the outlines of a correct and more developed approach to the problem are discernible.

[19] In *Non abbiamo bisogno*, AAS 25 (1931), Pius XI defended a true 'liberty of conscience'.

[20] E.g. 'Messagio di Natali', 1942, AAS 37 (1943).

[21] 'Allocuzione ai giuristi cattolici Italiani', 6 December 1953, AAS 20 (1954).

D

harmony with the dignity of the individual person in the present supernatural order, the competence of the State and the mission of the Church. And while no papal statement has given clear and full recognition to this position, it has the growing support of theologians all over the world, it has been espoused by eminent members of the magisterium,[22] and it is very much in the spirit of statements by Pius XI and Pius XII.

Such a solution would be of great help in reducing tension between the Catholic Church and the other Christian bodies. It would not banish overnight the prejudices of a Blanshard, but it would be a much needed counter to his propaganda. And it would give new understanding and encouragement to a Pelikan or Albornoz.

The problem of religious freedom and the State has been too long divisive amongst Christians, too long an obstacle to their mutual understanding and to their common struggle for man and man's freedom against the enslaving powers that threaten him. And – to complete the tragedy – it may have been quite unnecessary. A theology of religious freedom that accepts the value of truth, that defends man's right to seek and live that truth, that regards religious truth and life as superior to State authority, while recognising the legitimate claims of that authority to uphold public order and morality, has much to commend it to all Christians and may yet prove a bond between them.

---

[22] Cf. C. Journet, *Droit de la vraie religion et tolérance civile des cultes* in *Nova et Vetera*, 26 (191), no. 1, 6 ff., and Carillo de Albornoz, op. cit., 13 ff. The recent, comprehensive statement by the Cardinal and bishops of Tanganyika on the problems of a pluralist society is an excellent outline of the solution which is favoured here. Cf. *Documentation Catholique*, 15 October 1961, cc. 1298-1305; 5 November 1961, cc. 1395-1405.

What for so long has divided us may yet in God's providence help to unite us. This unnecessary obstacle may yet disappear to give way to a fuller understanding of the truth of Christ by all of us.

6. Tolerance[1]

Tolerance is not a new problem. It is at least as old as the first sin. For the problem of tolerance is the problem of living together, or rather an attempt to solve the problem of people living together in peace and harmony despite their differences. And it is a problem that affects every level of human living. It is a family as well as an international problem, a problem for the village community as well as the State, for the presbytery, religious house or parish as well as the universal Church. Wherever there are people living together, there is continuous demand for the exercise of tolerance.

This problem of living together, of co-existence in the current cliché, has received a new urgency to-day when the only alternative to interracial and international tolerance may be total war. But at this, as at every other level, the problem is essentially personal. It is caused by the meeting of different persons and it can be properly solved only by an appreciation of the value of the person.

The Dignity of Man

Man, God's masterpiece, is at once the climax and the

[1] First published in *The Furrow*, January 1961.

master of physical creation. As an animal he is its climax in the extraordinary complexity of his living organism. While the most rudimentary human cells remain a mystery to man and the nucleus baffles his attempt to express nature in a formula, the mystery of the human body should inspire reverence and wonder as the most remarkable physical manifestation of the perfection and power of the Creator.

Man is at once part of and above the physical creation. It is by his share in the spirituality of God that he properly manifests the divine perfection. It is by his spiritual powers of intellect and will that he shares in the divine guidance of the world. It is as a person, a knowing and loving being, that he is the master of creation. But we have not yet reached the full measure of his worth and dignity. God has called this person to a destiny far beyond his natural capacity, to a direct personal union with Himself in the intimate knowledge and love of the life of the Trinity. And He has offered him a first instalment of that union here on earth through the infusion of sanctifying grace.

The manner of this offer is no less remarkable. God's long and patient attempts to woo man to this union of love with Himself, after man had rejected God's first offer, is an indication in itself of the value of the person in God's estimation. This divine courtship, which despite the continued unfaithfulness we find recorded in the Old Testament, culminated in the espousals of the Incarnation, when the Son of God by the consent of the Virgin and through the power of the Holy Ghost, became the Son of Man. God became man to lead man back to God. Even this extraordinary gesture was misunderstood by God's own chosen people. It took the suffering and death of the God-man to achieve the reconciliation and to enable man to enter again into that love-relationship to which God calls him, continuously and by name. In His anxiety to protect man's personal gifts of intellect and will, God never forces an entry; He stands at the door of each man's heart and knocks, awaiting the invitation to enter.

The divine generosity in endowing man with his spiritual powers and in giving him this personal call to union places an extraordinary responsibility on each individual to answer this call freely, to return love for love. And the consequences of refusal are incalculable. The first charge of each man then is to use his spiritual powers of intellect and will to seek to know and love his Creator, to seek the truth and to live by it. And it is the duty of every other individual and of every group to respect this.

Justice

This is a matter of justice, of giving a man his strict due, based on a recognition of his essential worth as a person. To attempt to impose any creed, even the true one, by force is directly to violate this right. It is a devaluation of the person and contrary to divine example and precept. Into the intimate recesses of a man's mind, as he seeks after the truth, no human authority may forcibly intrude, when God Himself stands at the threshold and waits. The various attempts, past and present, to solve the problem of living together by imposing uniformity of belief are a denial of man's dignity as a person. And because man's consciousness of his dignity is so deeply rooted in him by God Himself, the solution is inevitably impermanent.

To grow and develop as a person man needs the help of his fellow man. He needs society. Society means order, authority, law. Subjection to authority and law is of necessity limiting for man: he will be forbidden certain activities, restrained if he attempts them and punished if he carries them out. And all this is willed by God in order that man may develop as a person. Human society then and human law are intended to protect man's personal gifts of knowledge and freedom and to promote their development. Laws which disregard his nature and value as a person are contrary to the divine purpose of society and unjust. But because he could not function or develop without society, man must cherish in his turn the values of that society. He must honour its authority as coming ultimately from God and conform to its just laws. The exaggeration of individuality which ignores man's social nature leads to anarchy and the destruction of personal values.

It is in the fair administration of just law, based on a correct appreciation of the human person and of human society that the necessary groundwork for harmonious living is laid. Unfortunately the proper balance between the rights of the person and of society is a difficult one to strike and still more difficult to maintain. There has always been a tendency for the central authority to extend its powers, a tendency greatly facilitated in modern times by technical progress in communications and arms. The growth in the complexity of modern life joined with these new technical developments are a strong source of temptation to government powers, who are often too willing to believe that they can order human life better by ordering it more. Democratic governments, however, still believe in the worth of the human person whom they should serve. For the completely totalitarian State the value of the person is his value to the State. What God created as an end becomes for this State a means. The person is compelled to serve the State and the divine order is reversed. Thus the totalitarian solution to the problem of living together is to deny personal rights and values and subordinate all to the demands of the State. It is the solution of complete intolerance.

There are other, less radical, forms of the intolerance solution, where the State on the basis of creed, colour or class unjustly restricts the rights of certain citizens. Many painful examples of this intolerance come to mind. It is based on an exaggerated notion of the State's competence and a consequent devaluation of the person. This is particularly true of the most painful of all forms of intolerance, that inflicted by the State in the name of religion. Religious freedom in the State is one of the most delicate and explosive aspects of the tolerance problem. Here we can only suggest the broad lines of a solution.

The State is a natural society. Its purpose is to promote man's natural perfection by promoting the public welfare or common good. The private beliefs of the citizens are not the concern of the State authority, until they are given public expression and affect that public order and morality which the State is bound to uphold. Private acts of immorality which have no social consequences do not impinge on society and are not subject to the authority of the State. The State's duty is to punish crime, not private sins. This public morality which the State must uphold is ideally identical with the morality of the Natural Law, which is the source of the State itself. In particular circumstances public morality may be less than that of the Natural Law. State legislation, as Saint Thomas pointed out, must take account of the *mores* of the citizens and should not lay down rules which would not in fact be obeyed and would result in greater evils. So the State must in its laws sometimes tolerate departures from the Natural Law such as prostitution or the modern practice of divorce. When this toleration is necessary or desirable is frequently a very difficult question to decide.

Man is aided in his natural development by the State. He is also called to a supernatural life and destiny, in which he is aided not by the State but by the Church. In the religious field the State has no competence; it must leave the Church entirely free to carry out its spiritual mission. It may not therefore dictate or interfere with the religious beliefs of its citizens. The person has the duty and right to seek the truth about God and himself and to use the God-given help of the Church, when he recognises its divine origin. In this search for the truth or in his response to it as he sees it, he may not be impeded by the State. Any State interference to impose a creed on one whom God calls freely and who must respond freely to that call would be immoral on the part of the State, whose function is to provide those material and temporal conditions in which man can best come to God and His Church. Its duty is to uphold public order and morality, and protect the religious freedom of the individual and of the Church. Where, however, a particular religious sect or group violates public order or morality – by advocating, for example, ritual child sacrifice – it is the duty of the State to prevent it. Beyond these limits it has no competence.

The problem of religious tolerance in the State then reduces to recognising the worth of the individual, whom God freely calls to the true faith, the limits of the State's authority, in particular its incompetence in religious matters, and the mission of the Church. As a practical illustration of how these various elements are co-ordinated, no better example could be found than Article 44 of the Irish Constitution.

In solving this problem of living together, one must begin by recognising the strict rights of the person; what is his due in strict justice. This is demanded not merely of the State in its internal and external

activities. It is necessary to all ordered human relationships. Anything less than justice is intolerance.

Charity

Yet the mere observance of justice will not make
living together completely harmonious and satisfying.
Personal relations ask something more. It is charity,
love, which gives warmth and life to human society.
Justice is of value as a particular realisation of charity.

Charity is a recognition of the divine in man and a
movement towards it in love. It is an imitation of the
divine motion of love which issued in man's creation
and redemption. Personal relations with persons at
whatever level should be informed by this impulse of
charity. Even at the inter-nation level, the difficulties
of establishing an international rule of law based on
justice will be considerably eased when these are con-
fronted in a spirit of charity. When the dominant
idea is wishing well to others, helping the weaker
countries not merely for reasons of expediency but
out of a genuine interest in human welfare, there will
begin to develop the necessary atmosphere of trust.

There are certain guides for the exercise of charity.
The first is acknowledgement of sincerity. No matter
how radically the difference of opinions, one must
presume good faith. Insincere people will always be
found but insincerity is not to be presumed, if there is
to be any hope of living together in peace and charity
and of discussing differences in a rational manner.

In politics, accusations of bad faith, which can too
easily become part of the game, are a distinct handicap in seeking the community's welfare. In religion
such accusations and suspicions are more obviously
unworthy and harmful. It is a disturbing comment
on the scandals of a divided Christendom that Dr
Fisher should have to borrow the phraseology of

uneasy politics to say that the cold war between the Christian bodies was coming to an end and that the era of peaceful co-existence was at hand. Slowly and painfully, Christians are beginning to accept the sincerity of separated brethren.

Such acceptance is frequently called for within the Church of Christ itself. It can happen that one who is making a sincere effort to apply Catholic doctrine to the new circumstances of his time may have his good faith and motives impugned. Such a person may react to genuine criticism by like accusations. Unless sincerity is accepted at the outset, controversy will obscure rather than clarify; will give scandal rather than edification.

To the acceptance of good faith must be added, as a second guide in human relations, the recognition of what is good and true in a man and his views. Unless one recognises the good one cannot hope to love a man as God would have him loved. If no effort is made to understand the views of another and to see the truth in them, one cannot hope to have one's own views understood in turn. One of the great difficulties of living together is this problem of mutual understanding, of seeing what exactly our differences are so that we may respect and perhaps eventually remove them. The first task in any controversy, political or theological, is to understand the other man's terminology and grasp his position. Without such understanding no progress is possible.

This aspect of tolerance then is based on man's passion for truth, his desire to understand his fellow man and expound as clearly as possible the truths which he himself has accepted. Many who preached tolerance in the past were indifferent to truth, or at least to religious truth, a fact which causes some Catholics a certain uneasiness about tolerance, as if it necessarily involved minimising the truth.

The State's guarantee of freedom of religion is not a statement about the truth or falsehood of different religions. It need not, as we have seen, be based on indifference to religion. Similarly, the dialogue at present in progress between the different Christian bodies is not due to any spirit of indifference or calculated to promote such a spirit. It is a genuine seeking by men of goodwill for the reunion of all Christians in Christ's Church. In these efforts and prayers Catholics join wholeheartedly. They are conscious of the scandals and weaknesses of the divisions of Christendom and of their responsibility to help to heal them. They are anxious to understand and love their fellow Christians and pray that God may unite all men in truth and love.

Humility

In relations with other Christian bodies as in relations with all men, one must be ready to acknowledge one's share in the causes of estrangement. Humility is the third force, with justice and charity, in harmonious human living.

The constant experience of personal sins and sinfulness should be a reminder that whatever good is in us is from God, as it should prevent us from passing judgement upon the state of soul of our neighbour. For the good that is in us by the grace of God, we give thanks. We would share that good and truth with others but never in a 'holier-than-thou' attitude, which Christ criticised so severely in the Pharisees and which poisons genuine human relations. The incipient Pharisee in all of us, who surfaces in 'At least I didn't . . .' thoughts and remarks, needs constantly to be repressed if we are to remain realists, that is, humble before the truth.

Humility does not make men apologetic caricatures in society; it gives an ease and trust in social relations that the overbearing and the unsure never enjoy. Neither does it impede the due administration of human justice. It prevents rash judgement based on prejudice and lack of information and sets human justice in all its crudity in true perspective. Only God can judge the heart.

Standards are respected by the humble and tolerant man, who does not presume to judge the heart. He respects the divine in others while he is sharply aware when their work is defective. In criticism he will be seen to estimate the goodness of the work but his standards will be the accepted standards of good workmanship in that field and he will express with fairness the deficiencies he notes. And criticism must not only be honest and well intentioned. It must also be competent. The humble or tolerant man will not presume to offer criticism in a field in which he has no competence.

Living together in peace and harmony imposes then a considerable strain on mankind: it demands a combination of so many seemingly contradictory qualities. Respect for the rights of the individual must be reconciled with the demands of the community; charity towards all and acceptance of their sincerity with a passion for the truth; unwillingness in humility to judge others with the administration of human justice and the insistence on standards. Only a disciplined man possessed of a deep regard for the divine in human beings can combine so many and such diverse qualities. For tolerance is a characteristic not of the weak but of the strong; it is found in its fullness only in the Son of Man. All who would come after Him must submit to the discipline of the Cross, which tolerance involves.

7. Church and State in the Constitution of Ireland[1]

To cover the whole ground of the interplay of Church, understood as a religious denomination or as the Roman Catholic Church, and State, understood as the Republic or the whole of Ireland, would be unprofitable, if not impossible within the limits of this paper.[2] The Constitution reflects and directs the actual situation in this matter. Any criticism of the actual situation then must be based on an appreciation of the constitutional provisions.

The Constitution does not confine itself to a consideration of the Catholic Church and Catholic citizens. It could not. It must take account of all the citizens, Catholic and non-Catholic. Ireland taken as a whole or simply as the Republic is not an exclusively Catholic country. This paper must, in dealing with the constitutional provisions for religion and the Churches, take account of religions and denominations other than the Catholic. This is, as we shall see, essential to understanding the constitutional position.

Yet the emphasis will be on the position of the Catholic Church and its doctrinal demands. The effective ambit of the Constitution to-day is in a State

[1] First published in *The Irish Theological Quarterly*, April 1961.
[2] This paper was read at a meeting of Tuairim, London, 10 February 1961.

with a ninety-three per cent Catholic population. By Church-State relations people more frequently mean the relations between the Roman Catholic Church and the secular power. Witness the *Time* section on Religion and the theological prelude to the American presidential election. Catholic doctrine, as understood or misunderstood by Catholic and non-Catholic, is widely controverted, when it is not summarily condemned. And it is controverted not least amongst Catholic theologians themselves. As a Catholic priest I am qualified to speak only on the demands of Catholic doctrine and how the Irish Constitution meets them. For these reasons my paper will, as I said, devote much of its time to discovering what position the Catholic Church enjoys under the Constitution and to determining whether it meets the Church's doctrinal requirements.

After a brief word about the background to the Constitution and the historical influences which shaped it, my paper falls into two main parts. In the first part I examine the text of the Constitution to determine (*a*) its democratic character, and (*b*) its provision for religion and the Churches. In the second part I outline basic Catholic doctrine on Church-State relations and discuss whether the Irish Constitution meets those basic requirements while retaining its democratic character.

Historical Background

A Constitution is not, as you are well aware, a textbook of law, much less of political philosophy or theology. It is a crude, practical document laying down the fundamental law which is to guide a particular people in their concrete situation. It must take account of the character and needs of these people. It is influenced by their history and genius,

their hopes and fears – even their climate. It cannot
afford the precision and refinement of the textbook.
It is composed not *in vacuo* or in an air-conditioned
ivory tower, but in the sweaty political battlefield –
grappling with real problems and real people.

And in those sections of the Irish Constitution of
interest to us, there are, it seems to me, three historical
and local circumstances which had decisive influence.
To appreciate the aims and tendencies of the Constitution we must refer briefly to them here.

(1) The first and perhaps the most important of
these was the democratic and non-denominational
character of Irish political nationalism as it developed
in the nineteenth century and was inherited by Mr de
Valera's generation and by our own. The democratic
creed is a marked characteristic of the (Protestant)
father of Irish revolutionary nationalism, Wolfe Tone
and his United Irishmen. His argument on behalf of the
Catholics of Ireland takes the democratic line of the
equality of all men, Protestant, Dissenter and Catholic
as Irishmen. 'On what chapter of the Rights of Man
do we ground our title to liberty in the moment that
we are riveting the fetters of the wretched Roman
Catholics of Ireland.' Paine's book had great influence with Tone and his spiritual heirs. Davis and
Young Ireland, the Fenians, Sinn Fein and the men
of 1916 were insistent on the democratic character of
their hoped-for Irish State. And to this democratic
assurance they added express guarantees of religious
freedom for all and the exclusion of any discrimination
on religious grounds. The Irish constitutional movement was no less democratic in its utterances, at least
from the days of O'Connell, through Butt and Parnell
to Redmond. And their highest achievement, the
Home Rule Bill, carried similar guarantees of religious freedom. Both the revolutionary and constitutional movements counted Protestants and Presby-

terians amongst their most prominent leaders and friends. In practice as well as in theory both movements were strictly non-sectarian. Both streams of Irish political thinking then converged at least in their common attitude to democracy and religious freedom. This was the attitude which the founders of our State and composers of our Constitution inherited and found in their people.

But it would be a mistake to compare the strict non-sectarianism of Irish political theory and practice with the hostile or indifferent attitude to religion which was frequently the case in other countries.

(2) The second very important influence manifested in the Constitution is indeed the religious spirit of the Irish people. Many of the leaders of both the revolutionary and constitutional movements were themselves deeply religious men. And one of the striking characteristics of nineteenth century, as of twentieth century, Ireland is how the masses of the people remained faithful to their religion – and for the vast majority that was the Catholic religion. But this religious spirit was combined with a remarkable sensitivity to the distinction between politics and religion, between State authority and ecclesiastical authority. The popular reaction to the veto proposals, to directions from Rome on clerical participation in the Repeal movement, to the condemnation of the Plan of Campaign and so on, is sufficient witness to this.

(3) The final important influence – related to this distinction upheld by the laity – is the consistent attitude by the Irish hierarchy over two hundred years to relations with the civil authorities. In the days of British rule this attitude was one of respectful co-operation while reserving the right to criticise any Government measure on moral grounds and of persistent refusal to be in any way closely allied with the Government through official control or financial

endowment. The rejection of the veto even at the price of Catholic emancipation and in the teeth of the Roman directions and the repeated refusal to accept any State-endowment for the clergy, leaves no doubt that the hierarchy were determined to keep clear of any governmental patronage and control. And there is no evidence to suggest that any privileged position was sought, or would be accepted, under native government, although co-operation would naturally be more cordial.

With these three forces in mind, we go on to examine the actual text of the constitution.

Democratic Character of Constitution

The Constitution is, in general, that of a democratic state. Article 5 states that Ireland is a sovereign and democratic state. Article 6 states that all powers derive from the people and that they have the ultimate right to decide all questions of national policy in accordance with the requirements of the common good, i.e. of the people as a whole. In Article 15 and following, we have the provisions for a National Parliament which follows accepted democratic technique of governing through elected representatives. The Judiciary is independent of the Government. More important for us are Article 40 and following, which come under the general heading of 'Fundamental Rights'. Here the Constitution's democracy, as a way of guaranteeing the liberty and rights of the individual as distinct from a method of government, is put to the real test.

According to Article 40, Section 1, all citizens shall as human persons be held equal before the law. It is important to note that this equality of all before the law is based on their human personality and not on any grant from the state authority. Their equality as

persons antedates this State law. It is not granted, but
guaranteed by it. And the State guarantees in its laws
to respect and, as far as practicable, to defend and
uphold the personal rights of the citizen.

Section 4 of this Article and its various sub-sections
deal with the guarantee of personal liberty, of which
no man shall be deprived save in accordance with law.
Section 5 adds to this the guarantee of the inviolability
of the dwelling or home of every citizen.

The exercise of the three famous freedoms – of
expression, assembly and association – is guaranteed
under Section 6. But that exercise may not be unlimited, if society is to survive. So the freedoms are
subjected to the general requirements of public order
and morality which the Constitution demands that the
Irish State shall always uphold. The restrictions, however, imposed on the exercise of those rights for the
common good, to protect public order and morality,
shall, according to this Section, 'contain no political,
religious or class discrimination'.

The private individual's right to own external goods
is upheld in Article 43 and no law may be introduced
abolishing it. However, in the interests of the community as a whole, its exercise may be restricted.

In this respect for inalienable human rights the
Irish Constitution duly recognises the rights of the
family. The family, it declares, is the primary natural
unit-group in society and its rights are antecedent and
superior to all human law.

In education then, the rights of the parents are
basic. The State will try to help the parents to exercise
these rights effectively. It will, in the interest of
common good, insist on a certain minimal education
for all. But it cannot insist that for this education the
children attend a state school or indeed any school. And
it is very careful to respect scrupulously the rights of the
parents in the matter of religious and moral formation.

Whether you view democracy as a system of government of the people, by the people and for the people, or as a political system which guarantees the Rights of Man, the framework for the Irish State which the Constitution provides undoubtedly reflects the democratic character of Irish political nationalism.

Provision for Religion and the Churches

The Constitution reflects almost to a like degree what we have called the religious spirit of the Irish people. The Preamble, although it is no part of the Constitution proper, expresses the spirit of faith in which the Irish people approached this solemn task of adopting a Constitution. It reads: 'In the name of the most Holy Trinity, from whom is all authority and to whom, as our final end, all actions both of men and State must be referred, We, the people of Eire . . . do hereby adopt . . . this Constitution.'

In Article 6 God is acknowledged as the ultimate source of that authority which derives from the people. According to Article 44 God's name must be held in reverence. Blasphemy is, by Article 40, a criminal offence. Religion shall be duly respected and the State acknowledges that public worship is due to Almighty God. And the delicate reverence for the human person and his inalienable rights, which we have already observed, is a further indication of the State's respect for God's law and of its recognition of its own limitations.

It is in the provisions of Article 44, which comes at the end of the Section on Fundamental Rights and is in many ways its climax, that we find the final confrontation of the democratic and religious feelings of the Irish people. The introductory section about the State's duty to respect and honour religion has already been mentioned. The remaining sections deal (*a*) with the religion of the individual; (*b*) with the religious denominations or Churches.

The guarantee of freedom of conscience and of the profession and practice of religion is a natural conclusion to the earlier guarantees of freedom of expression, assembly and association. And it is expressed within the same limits – those of public order and morality. The further guarantee that the State shall not impose any disabilities or make any discrimination on the grounds of religious belief or status is a development of the earlier prescripts about the equality of all before the law. The Irish Constitution allows of no religious test for public office and many obvious examples of the effectiveness of this law come to mind.

Freedom of conscience and the equality of all before the law is not necessarily incompatible with special juridical privileges and support for a particular Church. This situation is not uncommon and is not confined to Catholic, or even Christian, countries. For us the most obvious example is in England, where the Church of England enjoys a certain juridical status as well as some financial support. In Italy the Catholic Church enjoys a similar position and freedom of conscience is guaranteed to all exactly as in England.

In Ireland it is not so. No Church is juridically privileged and the State is not allowed to endow any Church. At first sight this contention that there is no Church juridically privileged in Ireland might seem to be contradicted by the very words of Article 44, Section 1, Subsection 2: 'The State recognises the special position of the Holy Catholic Apostolic and Roman Church as the guardian of the faith professed by the great majority of the citizens.' Subsection 3, however goes on 'The State also recognises the Church of Ireland, the Presbyterian Church in Ireland, the Methodist Church in Ireland, . . . and the other re-

ligious denominations existing in Ireland at the date
of the coming into operation of this Constitution.'

These two sub-sections must be taken together in
the context of this particular Article and of the Constitution as a whole, if we would determine what this
special position and recognition mean. One opinion
maintains that the 'special position' recognised here is
a special juridical position, while the other denominations receive merely full toleration. What else can the
words 'special position' in a Constitution mean? And
why use two separate paragraphs – one for the Roman
Catholic Church and a second for the others?

This opinion is almost certainly false. What the
Constitution recognises is not any juridical position
but the social position of the Church, its position in
Irish society. It is recognising a fact – not a legal
privilege. This is the explanation advanced by Mr de
Valera in the Dail Debate in answer to a motion that
this clause about the 'special position' be deleted
because it did not confer any legal privilege on the
Church and was open to misinterpretation by un-
friendly critics. The Constitution should, Mr de
Valera said, recognise this very important social fact
which, because of the part religion played in Irish life,
would affect much of their legislation. The second
paragraph ensured the necessary freedom and equality
for the other religious bodies. The matter had been
carefully gone into, he added, and no objections had
been raised.

Since the coming into force of the Constitution no
Court has recognised any such legal status or privilege.
And the sharp lay and clerical reaction to some
extremists who wanted to have Article 44 altered so
that it would recognise the Catholic Church as the one
true Church and give it corresponding juridical status
never invoked the argument that it had already done
so. There is no basis for a distinction alluded to above

between 'recognition' for the Catholic Church and tolerance for all others. Even the very wording ('The State recognises the special position . . . The State also recognises the Church of Ireland') excludes it. And it would be opposed to the general spirit of the Constitution in its scrupulous guarantee of equal rights for all citizens irrespective of their religious affiliation.

In Section 2, Sub-section 2 the State guarantees not to endow any religion. And Sub-section 4 precludes any possibility of discrimination on religious grounds in providing State aid for schools. These normal adjuncts of a privileged Church are ruled out *a priori* by the Irish Constitution.

No one Church is privileged but all enjoy independence of the State in administering their own affairs. This is recognised by Sub-section 5. So is the right of each religious group to own and administer property, which property is granted special protection under the Constitution.

Freedom of religion for all within the limits of public order and morality, no legal privilege for any Church, but the recognition of the right of each to manage its own affairs – that is the position under Article 44.

There are, however, a couple of thorny problems affecting both Church and State which we must mention before we pass on to discuss the Constitution in the light of Catholic doctrine. The first of these – education – we have already touched on. In accordance with its democratic safeguard of the rights of the individual and family, the Irish Constitution recognises the rights of parents as basic. Accordingly, Catholic parents will be entitled to send their children to Catholic schools and to benefit proportionately from the public moneys spent on education.

On the question of marriage the Irish Constitution does not lay down any particular form of marriage as obligatory on all. So in practice a person may be

married in a registry office or by a religious minister in
a church. Individual freedom in this very sacred
matter is then expressly guaranteed. The State, however, pledges itself to safeguard marriage as the basis of
the family – the most important natural unit in society.
For this reason, no law allowing for a dissolution of
marriage may be introduced. If a marriage, which is
still valid in Irish law, is dissolved outside Ireland, the
partner to that marriage may not remarry in Ireland
while the other partner to that marriage is still alive.
And this applies to dissolution obtained at Rome, as
well as to civil divorce obtained in England or elsewhere. Accordingly, if a Catholic marriage is declared
null or dissolved at Rome, the partner may not remarry in Ireland, unless it is possible to prove the
marriage null in Irish law, although at least ninety-
three per cent of the people and Judiciary believe that
he is free to marry.

Although one must admire the courageous aims of
this Article, there are at least practical difficulties
about the Constitution's provision on marriage, from a
Roman and non-Roman point of view.

To sum up then – the Irish Constitution makes a
serious attempt to unite respect for religion and moral
values with democratic principles. From the democratic point of view of ensuring representative government and protecting the individual freedoms it has in
a large measure been successful. But how successful
has it been from the religious point of view – in particular from the point of view of the Catholic religion?
The second half of this paper is devoted to answering
that question.

Church-State Relations: Catholic Doctrine

Here we face an immediate and, to many people,
Roman and non-Roman, surprising difficulty, i.e.

that of determining what Catholic doctrine on Church-State relations is.

On reflection this is not very surprising. The Church did not come into the world with any well-defined set of principles for dealing with the State. Its own conception of its divine mission and constitution quickly brought it into conflict with the State authorities which had hitherto firmly regarded religion as part of their responsibility. The immediate struggle then was for survival – with little opportunity for careful elaboration of doctrine. Practical solutions, not doctrinal pronouncements, were the order of the day. In time the persecuting emperor became the protecting, and sometimes suffocating, emperor. And the character of the State with which the Church had to deal continued to change and develop. Frequently the Church's position was little more than the struggle for existence conducted now with the Holy Roman Empire and the feudal principalities, later with the emerging nation-states like the France of Philip the Fair, with the absolute Catholic monarchies of a Louis XIV or the hostile Protestant princes, with the revolutionary and liberal democracies of the nineteenth century and finally with the totalitarian régimes of our own time – Fascism, Nazism and Communism.

The nature of the Church has remained essentially unchanged, Her spiritual mission intact. But the nature of the State has changed. Its political mission and claims have varied. However, from a study of her own nature and mission, from a study of man's nature and of civil society, the Church has elaborated certain basic principles which she tries to put into practice in dealing with the different States and statesmen.

The discussion and clarification of these basic principles is still in progress. However, it seems to me that they can be reduced to three fundamental ideas or principles which are securely founded in Catholic doctrine and on which all Catholic writers today would agree, but about whose interpretation they would sharply differ. These three principles are: (1) The distinction and independence of Church and State. (2) The harmony that should exist between them. (3) The primacy of the spiritual.

I will give you my interpretation of each of these principles, an interpretation which is, I believe, well founded theologically and widely accepted in the Church today. I will then be in a position to see how far they are verified in the solution proposed in the Irish Constitution.

The distinction and independence of Church and State is easy to grasp. They differ in immediate origin – the Church was founded directly by the Son of God – the State springs from the nature of man. They differ in aim – the aim of the Church is the supernatural, eternal welfare of man, that of the State his natural and temporal welfare. And, of course, they differ in the means, supernatural and natural, which each must take to attain its end. Each is, however, necessary for man and each is supreme in its own order. In this order all other societies and individuals are subject to it.

This dualism which Christ hints at in His 'Render to Caesar the things that are Caesar's' becomes a fact with the foundation of the Church for man's eternal salvation, while his natural and temporal welfare remains subject to the civil powers which, St Paul says, all must obey and for conscience' sake. Pope Gelasius was the first to give the new duality of powers amongst men clear expression in his letter to Anastasius in the year 494: 'Two there are, O august emperor, by which this world is chiefly ruled: the sacred authority of the Popes and the royal power.'

Despite exaggerations in theory and practice by individual churchmen and statesmen, this distinction has persisted as the most significant part of Catholic doctrine on Church and State until it received classic exposition by Leo XIII:

> The Almighty, therefore, has appointed the charge of the human race between two powers, the ecclesiastical and civil, the one being set over divine and the other over human things. Each in its kind is supreme, each has fixed limits within which it is contained, limits which are defined by the nature and special object of the province of each, so that there is, we may say, an orbit traced out within which the action of each is brought into play by its own native right (*Immortale Dei*).

In introducing this dualism into human society, Christianity made an original and important contribution. Hitherto man's religious or spiritual and his natural or temporal welfare were subject to the one authority. The new distinction met with a great deal of resistance from the civil ruler who was unwilling to see his field of authority restricted or to recognise an equal and independent authority in spiritual things. And the distinction has been a source of tension, if not conflict, as each independent authority rejected what it considered encroachments by the other into its proper domain. Despite the ensuing tensions, we must accept the distinction as designed by God for man. And we can, in halting human fashion, see something of the wisdom of the design.

If the spiritual is to survive it must have some independence of the material and temporal. If man's eternal salvation is not to be lost sight of in the material political struggle for existence and development, it must be the charge of some authority freed from the immediate responsibilities of this struggle. Committed to a political authority able to subject the spiritual to its own ends or to a spiritual authority itself immersed in the political struggle, the spiritual and supernatural would gradually go under.

This dualism, as well as safeguarding the nature of the spiritual, provides much needed protection for the rights of the individual in the face of social authority. Whenever in the past the distinction was overlooked or denied by too close association of Church and State, or by subjection of one to the other, the freedom and rights of the individual were in some degree eclipsed. Witness the persecuting empire which denied the Church's independence: the too close association of Church and State under Charlemagne or in the high middle ages which gave us forced conversions and the Inquisition; the *cuius regio eius religio* principle which made the Protestant prince head of the local church and which was adopted by Catholic princes for their own political ends, leading to the penal laws in Ireland or the revocation of the Edict of Nantes in France; and in our own day the denial of religious and all basic human freedom in the totalitarian states of Nazism, Fascism and Communism. An independent Church is the best safeguard of man's inalienable and God-given rights against the increasing claims of the State. An independent civil authority is a real assurance for the individual against an intemperate and aggressive religious zeal.

Independent as they are, Church and State retain much in common. They have a common subject, the Catholic citizen, whose perfection or happiness they seek, although on different planes. They share a common ultimate origin, God, and are frequently concerned with the same human activities, although under different aspects admittedly. They cannot then avoid contact. To prevent that contact necessarily becoming conflict, against the manifest will of their ultimate founder and to the detriment of their common subject, some harmony between Church and State is obligatory.

This harmony must be based on respect for each other's autonomy. Any attempt by the State to regulate purely spiritual matters or any interference by the Church in purely political affairs would be opposed to such harmony and an immediate source of conflict. It is the responsibility of the authority in each society to promote as effectively as possible that good which is proper to it – the natural or supernatural good of its members.

The natural welfare of the citizens demands, first of all, peace and order. This is the first charge of the State. While preserving the peace and order it must seek to provide the means whereby the citizens can develop naturally. This natural development or perfection which the State seeks to promote is no mere material prosperity but the intellectual and moral as well as physical well-being of the citizen. It must, in the legal phrase, uphold public order and public morality, while it encourages and enables the citizens to grow and develop as persons on the natural plane. In doing all this, the State is co-operating in a very effective way with the Church because it is providing those conditions in which the Church can best make its message heard. Where poverty, ignorance and disease are widespread, above all where immorality and anarchy reign, the Church's purely spiritual message will lose much of its impact in the face of these urgent material needs. In recognising and guaranteeing the personal rights of the citizens in religion, education, marriage and so on, in other words, in recognising its own limitations, the State enables the Church to effect its transforming influence on society by its educational, charitable and pious works. This by divine institution is the Church's right which the State should not deny, but in recognising it the State is in reality promoting its own common good. A Church operating effectively in its sphere is of great help to the State.

We should beware of any confusion of the two orders. A good citizen or statesman may not be a good Catholic, or even a believer. And a good Christian is not necessarily a good citizen or statesman. But where the spiritual capital of society is low, where religion has little influence on the people, observation of law and promotion of the common good which should be based on justice and charity must be based on selfishness or mere whim. Social life becomes less stable. Selfseeking and irresponsibility lead to an increase in all kinds of crime. The States' task is made immeasurably more difficult, the citizen's position much less secure.

But how should such harmony, which is so obviously in the interests of Church and State, be given concrete expression? How should it be institutionalised or given juridical recognition? Here the controversy amongst Catholic theologians at once becomes acute. And the opinion which I favour is not yet universally accepted within the Church, although it is very widely accepted.

According to this opinion, no particular form of institutionalising this harmony between Church and State is demanded by Catholic doctrine. The form will vary from age to age and from State to State. It is not a matter of principle but of application of principle which must take account of the particular historical and local circumstances in which the principle of harmony is applied. In particular, according to this view, the form of application or institutionalisation which was known historically as establishment and which consisted in official State recognition of one religion as the religion of the State with various attendant privileges is not demanded by Catholic doctrine. It is not the one universally valid form of institutionalisation but a particular historical one which is in fact quite unsuitable in most countries today. Here the second opinion differs sharply from the first, which I have accepted. For the upholders of this second opinion establishment is the only correct application of the principle of harmony. Indeed it is part of the principle itself and must always be upheld where possible, that is, in countries with a Catholic majority. Anything less than establishment may be tolerated only as a temporary expedient.

It would take far too much time to enter into the theological merits of the dispute. Suffice it to say that in my view the second opinion is based on a confusion of principle with one historical application of principle, due to a misunderstanding of certain nineteenth century papal statements taken out of context and to a naïve respect for the value and necessity of juridical bonds.

According to the first opinion this harmony may take different institutional or constitutional forms. In a parliamentary democracy it may be sufficiently guaranteed in the recognition of the citizen's freedom and rights. Through acceptance and use of these rights Church and State may work harmoniously together.

Before I pass on from this second principle I must refer to one problem which has usually been associated with established Churches in the past and with the State's duty to co-operate with the Church – the problem of tolerance or religious freedom.

Civil intolerance, as you can see from the example of England, is not necessarily bound up with establishment. Neither is it, contrary to popular belief, a necessary feature of Catholic doctrine.

The State, as an institution of the natural law, must operate within its limits. It may not, therefore, impose any creed, religious or philosophical, on the citizens.

Man is free to seek the truth about himself, his origin and destiny. He is free to profess that truth and to live according to it. And even though what he professes is error, the State may not prevent him from professing that belief and from living according to it, except in so far as it violates public order and morality. An anarchist or a disrupter of public order must be restrained. So must the violator of public morality. Because the State springs from man's nature, the public morality which it is bound to uphold is ideally identical with the law of that nature. Due to man's weakness and sin, however, public morality or the morals generally received in a particular society may be something less than that. The State may then tolerate such public abuses of the natural law as prostitution where the prohibition of them, because of the people's weakness, would lead to greater evils. This is, strictly speaking, tolerance – the permission by the State of something which it could, strictly speaking, condemn. Recognition of the individual's right to profess and practise his religion, when it does not – as it normally will not – violate public order or morality, is quite different. The State has no authority over a man's religious beliefs and practices. Any interference by it would be an action outside its competence; it would be a denial of the freedom of the act of faith by which God freely calls man to Himself and man freely answers.

The harmony principle does not involve any discrimination against citizens of other faiths.

However this harmony is expressed, there will inevitably be moments of tension. To solve these difficulties Catholic writers invoke a third principle – the primacy of the spiritual. Because the end of the Church as man's supernatural welfare is superior to that of the State, the Church enjoys a certain primacy or superiority over the State. This, however, does not imply that the Church has any political authority over the State, any authority over the civil government as government. The Church's power is always spiritual, not political.

In regard to political activity as in regard to all human activity, the Church is an authoritative teacher of the moral law. So if she knows some human law to be contrary to that moral law, she may declare this law invalid. In regard to her own members, she can exact obedience to her rulings on the moral aspect of political activities. She can, for example, forbid them to join certain political organisations, because they have immoral ends in view or are using immoral means. The Church has then authority to interpret and teach the moral law and impose that teaching on her subjects. But she has no political authority over princes or governments as such. Wherever Popes exercised such authority in the past, its basis was not their papal supremacy in the Church but some other external and accidental ground.

The Constitution and Catholic Doctrine

We must now determine how far our three principles of distinction or independence, of harmony and of the primacy of the spiritual are verified in the Irish Constitution.

The distinction and independence seem obvious. By Article 5 Ireland is a sovereign and independent State. The government's authority derives (Article 6) from the people who alone are the final arbiters of national policy. And the powers of government are exercisable only by the Oireachtas as the duly recognised organ under the Constitution. The freedom of the Church to manage its own affairs is expressly guaranteed and the exclusion of any discrimination on

E

religious grounds prevents any possibility of confusion of the two societies.

In the Irish Constitution the societies of Church and State are distinct. But they are not opposed. The religious feelings which find expression in the Preamble are a reliable indication of the desire for harmony between Church and State which the Constitution manifests. By its careful recognition, in Article 6, of God as the ultimate source of the State's authority and by the recurring admission of the State's consequent limitations, i.e. in acknowledging those human rights which are inalienable and antecedent to all positive the law, the Constitution strictly confines activities of the State to its own proper sphere. Its further express recogniton of the Church's position in society and of her freedom to manage her own affairs provides the necessary basis for harmonious co-operation. And it is through the constitutional guarantees of the personal freedom of the individual, his freedom of expression, assembly and association, his part in choosing a government and influencing public opinion, and particularly through the recognition of the rights of parents in the matter of education, that the Church's teaching and transforming mission in society is assured.

There is no establishment – no recognition of the Catholic religion as a State religion. Harmony is sufficiently ensured without it.

And there is complete freedom of religion. The State will uphold public order and morality as it must, but beyond that it will not interfere with anybody's freedom in the profession and practice of religion or allow any discrimination on religious grounds. So, far from this freedom of religion disrupting the harmony which should exist between Church and State in Ireland, it promotes it.

And the primacy of the spiritual? It hardly seems

necessary to explain how this is verified in the Irish Constitution. Unless the Constitution were keenly aware of the superiority of man's religious and supernatural end to his natural end, harmony would in fact be impossible.

The religious spirit which pervades the Constitution and its recognition of the limitations of State authority by divine law, to which we have alluded, is ample witness of its recognition of the true hierarchy of values. And through the constitutional rights of Catholic citizens and statesmen the Church can use the influence of her teaching authority in moral questions.

The Irish Constitution is, in my opinion, a fairly successful union of democracy and Catholic teaching. It is by no means perfect – either in its democratic aspirations or in its adaption of Catholic teaching. Article 40, Section 4, Sub-section 1, for instance, on personal liberty, would be far from adequate in a mature democracy: 'No citizen shall be deprived of his personal liberty save in accordance with law.' Similarly, there would be dissatisfaction from Roman and non-Roman with particular aspects of Article 41 on marriage.

There are other criticisms which one might name. But, by and large, it is a splendid achievement and its general solution of the Church-State problem has much to offer to modern politicians and theologians in their search for a satisfactory formula. It is not an ideal solution to be copied by other States, even democratic States with Catholic majorities. But it is a sound application of the general principles of Catholic teaching to the Irish circumstances of the day.

8. The State's Obligation to Worship God[1]

The Conflicting Attitudes

In the controversy about Church-State relations which grew particularly sharp in the 1950s, one of the issues raised was that of the State's obligation to worship God. But despite the development in understanding of Catholic doctrine on the State and especially in its duties in regard to religious freedom to which the controversy led, this notion of the State's obligation to worship did not benefit by any corresponding clarification.

The debate concerned the basic principles of Catholic teaching on relations between Church and State, in particular whether or no the State had an obligation in principle to recognise legally the religion of the Catholic Church as the religion of the State. Those who taught that the State had such an obligation in principle frequently argued in the following manner:

The State has an obligation to worship God.

But it must worship God in the manner in which God willed to be worshipped, i.e. in the rites and liturgy of the Catholic Church.

[1] First published in *The Irish Theological Quarterly*, April 1963.

Therefore it must legally recognise the Catholic Church as the State-Church, i.e. in which the State at least fulfils its obligations of worship.

This argument derived from the State's obligations to worship God was not the only argument used. But it was considered a very important argument. And it was spelled out with considerable emphasis in that area where the controversy was at its sharpest – in the United States.[2]

To prove the State's obligation to worship God, its defenders like G. W. Shea[3] advance arguments from reason and authority, arguments common to the other major supporters of that position, the authors of the manuals of public ecclesiastical law as well as to many manuals on the theology of the Church.

And the opponents of the Catholic-State thesis as it was called do not reply by any denial of the major or indeed any extensive analysis of it. They are not concerned then primarily with the State's obligation to worship God. They simply deny that it can lead to the conclusion which Father Shea deduces from it, the obligation of the State to establish the Catholic Church as the State-Church. They prefer to approach the problem in more general terms by discussing the nature and purpose of both Church and State and deriving from these the basic principles governing them, which do not in their view include legal recognition. The State's obligation to worship causes a certain unease because of its form of expression but it is not denied and it would in the view of Father Murray, to specify more precisely Father Shea's major opponent, be automatically fulfilled in a predominantly Catholic

[2] Cf. Shea, G. W., *Catholic Doctrine and the Religion of the State* in *Am. Ecc. Rev.*, 123 (September 1961), 164 ff.
[3] Loc. cit.

State 'by religious acts performed on State occasions'.[4] However, no fuller analysis of the meaning and extent of the State's obligation or of the validity of the arguments on which it is based is attempted.

The continuance of the controversy in the succeeding years has led to some fuller examination of this obligation of the State to worship. This examination was carried out in some detail by the Spaniard Jimenez et Urresti in a doctorate thesis presented at Rome in 1958. Writing within the school represented by Father Shea, which demands official recognition of the Church as a matter of principle, he does not seem to demand worship in the strict sense of formal ritual acts of worship from the State.[5] Accepting the fundamental principles of the same school, if applying them in a modified form, J. Newman maintains that the State can worship in that 'each citizen *qua* citizen and each ruler *qua* ruler can render personal acts of worship to God'.[6] Another moderate defender of this general position, the Italian G. Picchieri, demands such ritual worship from the State through the presence of its representatives at worship on special national occasions.[7]

[4] Cf. Murray, J. C., *The Problem of the Religion of the State* in *Am. Ecc. Rev.*, 124 (May 1951), 342. Father Murray's extended treatment of Church–State relations and his analysis of Leo XIII are contained for the most part in *Theological Studies*, 1945–1955. It is difficult to be sure of Father Murray's exact position in this point. But Father Shea (art. cit. 165) claims that he concedes this obligation and Father Murray does not deny that, although he has obvious misgivings about the expression.

[5] Jiminez et Urresti, Theodorus Ign., *Estado e Iglesia*, Rome 1958, 383 ff. He denies an obligation of ritual worship but admits that acknowledgment of God implicit in obeying the moral law, etc. This is to some extent based on his distinguishing the State from the authorities.

[6] Newman, J., *Studies in Political Morality*, Dublin 1962, 284.

[7] Picchierri, G., *Confessionalità e laicità d'uno stato moderno* in Rivista di pedagogia e scienze religiose, I–1 (1963), 60 (January–April 1963).

A very different attitude is manifest in the letter published by the hierarchy of Tanganyika on the occasion of its independence. It denied the State the right to establish one religion but it did insist on the State's care for religion and the need for co-operation between Church and State.[8] And if representatives of State because of its symbolic role choose to participate occasionally in religious ceremonies, their action is a praiseworthy one. This is a far cry from the State's obligation to worship and consequent obligation to establish the Catholic Church.

However, a more radical note still is struck by Archbishop Hurley of Durban in his artiels *The Church-State Dilemma*. From the difficulties raced by the 'traditional' argument for special recognition for the Church based on the State's obligation so worship God, 'there is only one escape . . . and that it to admit that the State has no religious obligations whatsoever under the New Testament'.[9]

Here then are the conflicting positions – the State has an obligation to worship God and therefore to recognise the Catholic Church as the State Church (Shea), the State may be said to have an obligation to worship God but no consequent obligation to recognise the Catholic Church in this way (Murray), the State has an obligation to recognise the Catholic Church but not to worship in the strict sense (Jiminez et Urresti), the State has no right and of course no obligation to recognise any religion as the official religion but its participation by its representative at worship is praiseworthy (the Bishops of Tanganyika), the State has no obligation to recognise the Church or

[8] *Les problèmes posés par une société pluraliste. Lettre collective de l'Episcopat du Tanganyika* in Doc. Cath., 58/1363 (5 November 1961), col. 1399.

[9] Hurley, Denis E., *The Church–State Dilemma* in The Furrow 14/3 (March 1963), 144.

to worship (Archbishop Hurley). From which some analysis of the meaning and basis of the proposition 'the State must worship God' seems imperative.

Much of the confusion which has arisen must be attributed to inadequate or divergent understandings of the two terms *state* and *worship* in this proposition.

Meaning of State

The difficulties surrounding the term *state* may be traced for our purposes to Christ's institution of the Church. When He commissioned His apostles to carry on his supernatural work of salvation independently of the civil or political authority, He introduced a dichotomy into man and society which was revolutionary in its time. The civil powers were left in charge of civil or political affairs, the affairs of Caesar,[10] and in these matters they were to be obeyed for conscience' sake, as deriving their power ultimately from God.[11] But man's religious, supernatural and eternal welfare was the responsibility of a new and independent authority and it found social expression and development in a distinct religious society, the Church.

The implications of this revolutionary change could not be completely grasped and expressed at once. 'The Church did not come into the world with a ready-made doctrine to govern her relations with secular powers.'[12] It was only gradually and often at great cost to herself that she was able to uphold her basic right of freedom to preach Christ's message to mankind. The further implications of this freedom were later recognised and to some extent realised in different ways in different parts of the world and at different

[10] Matt. 22:21.   [11] Rom. 13:1-5.
[12] Lecler, J., *The Two Sovereignties* (E. tr. *L'Eglise et la souverainité de l'État*), London 1952, 51.

times. But the important point to note here is that the institution of the Church and its gradual recognition and realisation of its rights must form the obvious starting point for a discussion of the nature and scope of the civil authority and so of whatever was later described as the State.

The civil authority is now restricted to promoting the temporal welfare of man. For it, this was the first important consequence of Christianity. What exactly that implies has been the subject of dispute and development. It has varied at different times with different countries and different forms of government. But it is now widely accepted even by politicians and political theorists who would deny the Christian origins of the theory, that the business of the civil power is solely the temporal welfare of the people whom it serves.

A second source of difficulty and confusion has been the growth in understanding the nature of civil authority itself, its manner of exercise and its relation to the people whom it governs. This development has frequently strayed beyond the bounds of the purely temporal to which it should now be restricted. Such straying cannot be accepted as justified. But even within these bounds there has been considerable development from the Roman Emperors through Feudalism, the Nation States, the Absolute Monarchs to the multiplicity of modern forms ranging from totalitarian dictatorships to constitutional democracy in its various degrees.

Despite the variety of institution and exercise which this civil authority has assumed, we can point to a certain definite development which seems irreversible although by no means complete. And it is in describing this developed understanding of the political authority and its relation to the people whom it serves that we may be able to isolate some definite meaning for the term *state* and so arrive at some idea of its *obligations* to God.

A community or group of people bound together by a common territory, history, etc., forms itself into a political society when it adopts some supreme authority in the group with the special task of looking after the common (temporal) welfare of the whole group.[13] How it does that will vary considerably. But certain elements seem clearly demanded. The authority comes from the group because it is their welfare which it must promote. The authority is vested in certain institutions, e.g. a monarchy or a parliament with courts and an administrative service. And it is vested in them for certain precise purposes, contained in the temporal common good. The exact definition of these purposes will depend on the needs and demands of the group. But there are certain limits. The maximum limit excludes the religious and supernatural welfare although it includes moral welfare, the minimum limit demands at least peace and order within the group and defence against attacks from without.

After this elementary description of the reality it may be possible to introduce and define some terms. The people who organise themselves under these institutions of authority to achieve the temporal common welfare are, as organised in this way, frequently described as the 'body-politic'.[14] The common good at this level is called the political good, the institutions charged with seeking it political institutions, (some of) the men who operate these institutions politicians and so the whole body of people as organised under these institutions the body politic. Individual members of the body politic are called citizens.

Many people use other terms for the people or community organised in this way. The civil or political

[13] Cf. Maritain, G., *Man and the State*, London 1954, *passim*.
[14] Cf. Maritain, o.c.

society is sometimes used. So is the term *state*. In fact,
since the end of the nineteenth century the word *state*
has been used very frequently for this reality. Such a
usage is justified, provided one is quite clear on its
meaning – the community as organised by political
institutions for the political end of promoting their
common temporal welfare. And here it is necessary to
distinguish the community as politically organised in
this way from the community organised in other ways.
The body-politic is the supreme organisation in the
temporal order, but it is not the only one. It does not
exhaust the social or society life of man even in the
non-religious field. And Catholic thinkers have consistently refused to identify the State or body-politic
with society, with all the manifestations of man's social
nature on the temporal plane. That forms the basis of
much Catholic social directive, as expressed for instance
in the principle of subsidiarity. The political organisation and its institution govern but they do not
extinguish the other social activities and organisations
of the citizens.

Here then is one definite meaning for the word *state*,
the body-politic, the people as they are organised, by
their political institutions for the common good.

It is these institutions themselves which provide the
form of the State, which constitute the people a body-
politic. They are established in various ways through
a gradual historical process or at one moment by the
declaration of independence and the adoption of a
constitution, as happens frequently in the former
colonies of Africa today. Because they institute the
people into a distinct political entity, and have been
devised by the people to provide directly for the common welfare, these institutions are nowadays frequently
described by writers as the State.[15] For these writers
these institutions should be distinguished from the

[15] Cf. Maritain, o.c., Murray, o.c.

body-politic, which is a group of people not a set of
institutions. They are superior to the body-politic as
empowered to direct and govern it for the temporal
welfare. But they are in a basic sense inferior to it as its
instrument and as devised by its choice and continuing by its consent. The body-politic may change
these institutions if it finds them unsuited to the purpose for which they were designed.

Because these two entities are so diverse, it is con-
fusing to say the least they they should be, as they
sometimes are, described by the one term, *state*, even
if this term is further qualified in the expressions
state-community and state-authority.[16]

The inadequacy of this qualification appears as
soon as you introduce the further necessary distinction
between the institutions of State and the people who
are operating them. The institutions themselves are
permanent machinery for the political task of promoting the common good through what are now distinguished as legislative, administrative and judicial
activities. And the people who are operating them,
particularly the people who discharge the legislative
function, are also sometimes described as the State,
at least when discussing the State's obligation to
worship God.

There are then three distinct entities described as
State in the writing on this subject – the body-politic,
the political institutions and the people who operate
these. It is very desirable that the State should be confined to one of them. But until by common consent
that is achieved, to solve our problem, it is necessary
to take each of these in turn and examine what it
means to say that the State must worship God. Before
turning to that task, however, it will be useful to discuss the meaning of worship.

[16] Cf. Shea, loc. cit., Picchieri, loc. cit.

Meaning of Worship

Worship or cultus[17] may be defined as showing of
reverence or honour to a superior. It is a recognition
of the superior's excellence formally expressed to him.
When that superior is God, the expression may of
course be purely internal. However, as man is not a
pure spirit but also a physical and social being, it
seems reasonable that the worship would be expressed
externally, through physical gestures in act or word
and socially in an organised community activity. And
the worship which God has imposed on man finds this
external, social quality in the ritual worship of the
Catholic Church. In the Church, as a member of it,
assisting at its liturgical services man expresses his
acknowledgement of God's excellence externally and
socially. He fulfils his duty of public worship as it is
called.

God's excellence and superiority are acknowledged
by man implicitly in a thousand ways, indeed in all his
activity. Where man in his activity takes account of
God's law, thereby recognising the divine superiority
and man's dependence on him in this sphere also, man
is implicitly paying tribute to God's law and may in
this broad sense be said to be implicitly or virtually
worshipping God.[18] Such a usage is however rather
loose and not what is meant by those who claim that
the State must worship God as Father Shea insists.[19]

[17] Cf. S. Th. 2a, 2ae, q. 81 a. 1, 2.
[18] Saint Thomas distinguishes worship in the strict sense as
elicited acts of the virtue of religion and that in the broad sense
as commanded acts of that virtue. S. Th. 2a, 2ae, q. 81, a. 1 ad 1.
[19] Loc. cit., 'To satisfy its religious obligations, the State must
worship God not only indirectly, virtually and administratively,
but also directly and formally. That is to say, not only, for
example, by abstaining from whatever is contrary to divine law
but also by official participation in acts of worship properly so-
called – of adoration, thanksgiving, supplication and the like.'

But what is meant? Worship may be confined for the present to its strict sense, formal recognition of the divine excellence through the acts usually associated with this, adoration, thanksgiving, petition. And as we are dealing with the State, a social entity in all its various senses, the worship in question is public or social, performed by public ritual acts and prayers.

The State and Worship in the Strict Sense

Where the State is taken as the body-politic, the whole people politically organised in pursuit of their common temporal welfare, in what sense can you speak of it as worshipping or having an obligation to worship God? It is difficult to see how in many States the people as a whole could be got together to express formal worship of God. And if they could in a small city republic, for instance, have they an obligation as organised politically to do so? Their political organisation seeks the temporal welfare. It must in the Christian context explicitly exclude their religious welfare, that belongs to a separate authority and separate organisation, the Church. As a member of political society each man is *qua* citizen bound to seek the common temporal welfare by obeying the just laws of the political authority and fulfilling his civic duties. That is the scope and the limit of his duties as a citizen. And he must in discharging them be aware of the higher law, God's law, which governs all men's activity. But he has no duty *qua* citizen to worship God, privately or publicly. That duty he has as a man and as a Christian. It is not a civic duty. Of course he will as a man and a Christian submit all his activity to God, ask Him to bless it and thank Him when success crowns his efforts. And this of course includes political or civic activity. And he should do this externally and socially but in the manner and social institution provided for him by God, in the liturgy of the Church.

It does not seem then that the activity of the State as body-politic taken as a whole or of its individual members can include liturgical worship of God within its scope. To do so would blur the distinction which Christ introduced between the two powers and two institutions. Man's civic activity is, of course, subject to God and his law, but it does not include worship. That worship is of obligation for man but it is fulfilled in his other great sphere of activity, the religious sphere, now organised and exercised in the Church.

If the body-politic has no such obligation, clearly the institutions by which it is constituted will have none. In any case they are not persons but institutions and could not simply participate in acts of worship. Perhaps the persons who manage them on behalf of the body could! A common explanation of the expression 'the State must worship God' is that the chief officials of State should take part from time to time in acts of worship in their capacity as chief officials.[20] But their capacity as political officials does not go beyond the political. Their mandate from the people to pro- mote the temporal common good does not include representing the people in acts of worship. The people have their own representatives in this matter, those given them by God, the priests of the Catholic Church.

The political officials will discharge their political office in accordance with their mandate expressed in the institutions which they operate and subject to the law of God. They will themselves, as men and as Christians, invoke God's blessing and guidance for the successful carrying out of their serious responsibilities. And like all men they have an obligation to worship God and in the forms of the Catholic Church but that

[20] Cf. Shea, Newman, Piccieri, etc., loc. cit.

obligation does not arise from their capacity as servants of the body-politic but from their destiny as men.

Yet certain offices in the body-politic and the men who fill them acquire a symbolic value. So it is praiseworthy and desirable that the harmonious relations which should exist between the two supreme powers on earth, the political and ecclesiastical, should be given symbolic as well as real expression. The real expression consists in respecting each other's independence and integrity as well as in harmonious co-operation in matters which affect both vitally, such as public morality, education and marriage. The symbolic expression may consist in the religious leaders invoking special blessings on the work of the political by the provision of special Mass at the opening of parliament or other State occasions at which the political leaders may be received with special formality. The courtesy is reciprocated and the symbol repeated when the political authorities provide a civic reception for notable Church dignitaries and so on. These symbolic actions are desirable for the furtherance of harmony but they are not, in any of the senses of State which we have seen, or in the proper sense of worship, acts of worship by the State.

God and Political Activity

The conclusions that the State has no obligation to worship God in the strict sense of worship may be more precisely expressed by saying that political activity, the activity of the body politic as such through its institutions and representatives or of the individual citizens as citizens, does not include such acts of worship. This may not be taken to mean of course that the people in their political activity, i.e. in the State, are not dependent on God and His laws and must not acknowledge this dependence. In seeking his temporal common good through political activity, man must respect his God-given nature and its laws as well as the higher destiny to which he has been called. The first he achieves through ensuring that his political activity and the laws in which it issues are in harmony with the divine law of his nature, the second through confining this activity to its purely temporal field and ensuring thereby the other divine power of the Church the freedom to cater for man's religious needs, to provide for his obligation to worship and to draw him towards his eternal and supernatural destiny. By keeping its laws and activity in harmony with the divine natural law and providing in this way for the activity (including worship) of the Church, the body-politic, its political institutions and representatives acknowledge in the only way possible to them the superiority and excellence of God. Sometimes one finds this activity described as virtual or indirect worship of God. But it is not what is usually meant by State-worship of God. It would perhaps be in the interests of clarity to use worship only for worship in the strict sense. Where, however, it is used in a wider sense in present-day or past writing, that must be clearly understood.

The Arguments for the State's Obligation to Worship

It is now necessary to comment, at least briefly, on the main arguments advanced in support of the proposition 'The State must worship God'. The analysis of the proposition already presented makes lengthy comment less necessary, at least for the arguments from reason and nature. And to do complete justice to the arguments from authority would require a separate article.

From Reason

The argument from reason is presented in one of two forms.[21] They are, however, frequently combined as developments of the one argument. The first of these is based on the social nature of man. That demands that he worship God socially, in society. So, the argument goes, he should worship Him in the supreme natural society, the State. Accordingly, he must as a member of the State, and the State must as the supreme social manifestation of man, worship God by social acts of worship in the strict sense. This argument ignores the nature and limitation of the body-politic and its political activity, and the related fact that in the Christian era man's social worship finds expression in a distinct society, that of the Church. Of course man has an obligation to social worship. But he fulfils it not in the State but in the Church. As a member of the body-politic he seeks the temporal welfare of all. His activity is political. As a member of the Church he seeks his supernatural destiny and performs his ritual acts of worship publicly and socially. He is the same man with civic and religious obligations which should not conflict but do not coincide.

A second form of the argument says that a State is dependent on God. It is sometimes described as a creature of God. (This tendency to make it into a substance distinct from the persons which compose it has been at the root of much of the confusion.) As a creature, dependent on God, it must acknowledge this and must acknowledge it by ritual acts of worship which will be performed by its representatives as only physical persons can actually perform these.

The State taken as the body-politic depends ulti-

---

[21] Cf. Shea, loc. cit., where he quotes the various authors who present their arguments in this manner.

mately on God as deriving from man's God-given social
nature. In its activity it should acknowledge this but
in a way proper to itself which is the way of political
activity in harmony with the divine law. Political
activity is the characteristic activity of man as a
citizen and of the body-politic as a political organisation and it is only by this proper activity that the
acknowledgement of God can be made. Formal acts
of worship do not form part of this activity. They do
not come within the scope of man's political organisation. For this organisation or activity does not exhaust his potentialities or duties even socially. His
religious potentialities and duties are now exercised
and exercised socially in the Church. If the political
society were the sole expression of man's social life
or if it were the society which had the responsibility
for his religious worship, then the argument based on
its dependence on God would have cogency in
establishing its duty of worship. As it is neither of
these, its dependence must, as we said, be expressed
in the manner and activity proper to itself, in its
political activity as in harmony with God's law.[22]

[22] The obligation of the State as a society to worship God is
stated in an interesting manner by Fenton, J. C., *Doctrine and
Tactic in Catholic Pronouncements on Church and State. Am. Ecc. Rev.*
145 (October 1961), 273–4, where he says 'objectively and apart
from all individual considerations, God deserves to be worshipped
by every individual and by every social unit, including the State,
according to the rite of the one true religion established and
sanctioned by Himself'. In an earlier article, *The Status of a
Controversy, Am. Ecc. Rev.* 124 (June 1951), 454, he speaks of 'the
obligation by which the State like every other society and every
individual being, is objectively bound to worship God according
to the precepts of the true religion'. It is hard to escape the
conclusion that the author maintains that every society, not just
the political society or the State, must worship God as a society
and therefore by social and ritual acts of worship. Does this mean
that, for instance, the Ford Motor Company, parent-teacher
organisations and the local golf clubs as 'societies' or 'social units'
must worship God? They are certainly dependent on Him and

State Worship and Freedom of Religion

There is one further point that might be made here
against the supporters of the State's obligation to
worship which may weigh at least with some of them.
Recent years have witnessed a remarkable development in the acceptance of the principle of religious
freedom. Writers who defend the State's obligation
to recognise juridically the Catholic religion, and to
worship God in its rite, would like to maintain that
this need not in any way interfere with the freedom of others to practise their religion and even
propagate it. But granted such formal recognition
and the acceptance of the State's obligation to worship, which means that the State official *qua* State
official and citizen *qua* citizen can and should worship
in the Catholic religion, then although the members
of other religions may be free to worship in their own
way, they cannot be admitted to complete citizenship.
They cannot exercise that civic right and duty of
worshipping as citizens or statesmen in the official
acts of worship of the State.

The Arguments from Authority

The arguments from authority in support of the
State's obligation to worship take again two main
forms, which however are very closely related. The
first involves the evidence of papal documents, the
other the continuous and common teaching of the

---

qualify for Monsignor Fenton's description 'society' or 'social
unit'. Such a conclusion helps to illustrate that while man has
an obligation to worship socially, it is not *qua* Ford employee,
qua golfer or *qua* citizen but *qua* man in natural law and *qua*
Christian in the New Testament economy. And this obligation
must be fulfilled in the Church.

theologians, canonists and moral philosophers in the
Church. Even a slight acquaintance with the theologians, etc., will show (*a*) how dependent those who
support the obligation are on the particular papal
documents,[23] (*b*) how divided they are today. The
value of their arguments from reason we have just
seen.

Papal Authority

The papal documents themselves reduce effectively
to the writings of Leo XIII. The passing references
culled from Pius X[24] and his successors do not discuss
the problem explicitly and provide no further elucidation of Leo's remarks. The encyclicals of Leo, especially the encyclical *Immortale Dei*, provide the am-
munition for the defenders of this position. It would
be impossible to make the necessary textual analysis
of all the relevant statements of Leo on this matter
and place them in the context of his complete writings
as well as in the historical setting to which they
belong. That has been attempted by people like
Father Murray,[25] Villatoux et Latreille[26] and Jienez

[23] A check of the major authors of Public Ecclesiastical Law
Manuals and of the other theologians and moral philosophers
listed for example by Father Shea loc. cit. reveals the very close
verbal similarity with which they repeat the arguments from
reason examined above which were regarded as the proper
interpretation of Leo XIII on the matter.

[24] Pius X, *Vehementer Nos*, Denz. 1955; Pius XI, *Quas Primas*,
Denz. 2196; Pius XII, *Summi Pontificatus*, AAS XXXI (1939),
420. These references to the recognition of God in man's social
and political life are more general in form than those of Leo XIII.
And while they are obviously dependent on his teaching they do
not clarify it or make it more precise, certainly not in the sense
of demanding worship in the strict sense from the State understood in any of its three senses.

[25] In a series of long articles in Theological Studies, 1952–53.

[26] *Christianisme et Laïcité* in Esprit, September 1950, quoted
Jienez y Urresti, o.c. 392.

y Urresti[27] with varying results.   Many others using the documents have been content to quote and prove.

It must be admitted then that the documents of Leo XIII provide problems of interpretation which have not yet been solved. But some indication can be given as to how the objections alleged from his writings to the position defended in this article may be met.

Two marked differences between Leo's treatment of the problem and any present-day treatment should be immediately noted. In the first place he was using a vocabulary and terminology in regard to political matters which is far less precise than that available to-day. He uses the expressions *societas civilis, societas, civitas, civilis communitas* and *natio* to refer in a general way to the temporal or natural order as distinct from the spiritual or supernatural as well as to the organisation of that order. He does not always clearly distinguish the political order within the wider social order or distinguish the body-politic from the wider society of which it is the political expression. He has a similar range of expressions for the authority in the temporal or natural order. So while he distinguishes very clearly between the religious, supernatural

---

[27] Op. cit., 383 ff., Jienez y Urresti is an interesting witness for a number of reasons. He is a Spaniard presenting a doctorate thesis at the Lateran University, Rome. It comes as no surprise then to find that he defends the thesis of the Catholic-state, the objective obligation of the State to recognise and profess the true religion. But he does not base this position on the argument that the State must worship God in the strict sense. In fact he denies that. And in support of his denial he presents the only extended textual analysis of Leo on this precise point which I have seen. The sense in which Leo demands as he does the State should *colere Deum*, may be, according to Jiminez et Urresti, in the sense of what Saint Thomas calls the *actus imperati virtutis religionis* as distinct from the *actus eliciti* (v. supra n. 18) and of what Father Shea calls worshipping 'indirectly, virtually and administratively' (v. supra n. 19).

authority of the Church and the civil authority and recognises the supremacy of each in its own sphere, he does not, as he could not at the time, define precisely the political order or body-politic. He does not distinguish it from the wider social grouping of the community or nation of which it was simply the political aspect. Similarly, in discussing the civil authority he did not distinguish as we would between the permanent institutions in which it was enshrined and the men who operated it.

A second important point to be remembered is the polemic context in which he was writing. He was defending the Church and its freedom, religion, its necessity and public character, against men who either denied these outright and wanted the civil authority to give this denial legal effect or who, if they admitted man's right to religion, confined it to the purely private and domestic sphere. Publicly, religion should not exist. Society and its authority did not recognise its existence.

Publicly and socially religion must exist as Leo was well aware. Society no less than the individual man must recognise that, because society no less than the individual owes its origin ultimately to God and depends on Him. This dependence must be acknowledged, it must be acknowledged publicly. And it must be acknowledged ritually. And society life cannot be conducted as if God did not exist.

What Leo was saying was undeniable. His manner of saying it was stamped with the strain of the polemic, a polemic against the spiritual heirs of men who had enthroned the Goddess of Reason in Notre Dame as symbolising the abolition of Christianity. The symbolic value of such gestures by men charged with the civil authority was clearly very important at the time. Because of the tradition which had gone before which had been a religious one, if often defective in other ways, Leo could not help contrasting the new attitude of the new authority with that of the old and defending the old.

The limitations in political terminology noted above and in a parallel understanding of the realities involved imposed certain limitations on Leo's expression also. The obligation of social worship, of worship by the community, etc., as described by him have not the precision which the further developments have made possible. In the light of these developments it is possible to understand and support Leo in his defence of public and social worship and in his rejection of the idea that body-politic, its authoritative institutions and their managers in seeking its temporal well-being, may behave as if God did not exist or religion were purely a private matter. But this social and community worship is not the eliciting of ritual acts by the body-politic or its representatives. Such social worship is exercised by man in the Church. And the acknowledgement of its dependence on God by the body-politic as such is accomplished in harmonising its own activity with His law.

The Theological Consensus

Finally, there remains the argument from the teaching of the theologians and canonists. This teaching stems almost exclusively from the encyclicals of Leo XIII and from an interpretation of his position that was understandable at the time but no longer convincing to-day. In itself it consisted largely in a repetition of the arguments from reason already discussed and a quotation from Leo, usually that from *Immortale Dei*.[28]

[28] The most quoted and quotable is the following section from *Immortale Dei*: 'Natura et ratio, quae iubet vel singulos sancteque religioseque Deum colere, quod in eius potestate sumus, et quod ab eo profecti ad eumdem reverti debemus, eadem lege adstringit

Neither by its age[29] nor its theological basis should it be described as the traditional teaching of the Church. The theological writing on this matter to-day has clarified and developed many of the points made by Leo. And this is no reason why development in the

civilem communitatem. Homines enim communi societate coniuncti nihilo sunt minus in Dei potestate quam singuli; neque minorem quam singuli gratiam Deo societas debet, quo auctore coaluit, cuius nutu conservatur, cuius beneficio innumerabilem bonorum, quibus affluit, copiam accepit. Quapropter sicut nemini licet sua adversus Deum officia negligere, officium est maximum amplecti et animo et moribus religionem, nec quam quisque maluerit, sed quam Deus iusserit quamque certis minimeque dubitandis indiciis unam ex omnibus veram esse constiterit, eodem modo civitates non possunt, citra scelus, gerere se, tamquam si Deus omnino non esset, aut curam religionis velut alienam nihilque profuturam abjicere aut asciscere de pluribus generibus indifferenter quod lubeat: omninoque debent enim in colendo numine morem usurpare modumque, quo coli se Deus ipse demonstravit velle'.

The word *colere* used by Leo XIII is of course capable of the two meanings mentioned by Jiminez et Urresti. And there is no difficulty in claiming that society, including political society, is dependent on God and must acknowledge that. But how? The development of the argument *sicut nemini licet sua adversus Deum officia negligere* just as no individual may neglect his duties to God but should embrace the true religion, etc., so in the same way *civitates* may not behave as if God did not exist. And in acknowledging His existence (*in eo colendo*) they must do it in the way which He wills. 'The way He wills' should be understood to refer not to the wider society, not to man then in general as a social being who must worship God socially in the Church, but to refer to the body-politic or its institutions which must 'worship' (*colere*) God in the only way possible to them, 'virtually, indirectly, administratively'. This second interpretation is favoured by Jiminez et Urresti and has much to commend it. But the lack of precision in Leo's writing in the matter is not confined to this use of *colere* but to an inadequate political vocabulary in regard to society in general and the various meanings of state. *Vide* text *infra*.

[29] The authors quoted in support of this view are all end of the nineteenth century or later, almost all writing after Leo and following what they believe to be Leonine teaching.

Church's thinking on Church-State relations should have stopped short at Leo any more than at Boniface VIII. To-day's development is in that traditional line and cannot be held to be opposed to the Church's tradition.

Conclusion

In analysing the proposition 'the State must worship God', it was necessary to define precisely what was meant by State. And this term is used by writers in this matter to refer to three distinct realities, firstly to that of body-politic or the people as politically organised to seek the common good, secondly to that of the permanent institutions by which they are so organised and thirdly to the officials who operate these institutions. The first reality, the body-politic, must also be distinguished from the wider community or society of which it is simply one aspect, the political. Worship, or what is relevant here, social worship of God, may be strictly defined as the social and ritual paying of honour to God in recognition of His excellence. Worship in the broad or improper sense is any implied recognition of this divine excellence and superiority in man's activity.

The State, taken either as body-politic or political institutions or the people who manage these, has no obligation to formal ritual worship. Its recognition of God's superiority is implicit in its own proper activity of promoting the political good. And man's obligation of social worship is fulfilled in the society given man by God for that, the Church.

This conclusion based on analysis of the terms and realities involved is confirmed by a consideration of the reasonable arguments advanced in support of the State's obligation to worship. And it is not invalidated by the arguments alleged from authority.

A final comment might be made in the desirability for clarity's sake of confining the disputed terms *state* and *worship* to one, strict, technical meaning, at least in this and related matters. For worship, that presents less difficulty. To restrict its meaning to formal and explicit acknowledgement of God's superiority through acts of adoration, praise, thanksgiving and petition, whether internal or external, private or public seems the proper course. In regard to the expression State, it would be more difficult to get unanimity. I myself favour the tendency of Father Murray to confine it to that set of institutions by which the people form themselves into a body-politic.[30] This is a definite reality which is aptly described by the term State and corresponds to the normal usage of the term in State-activity, State-owned property, State-laws, etc. And it has no other term by which it can be described, unlike the body-politic or the State-officials and government. With such a vocabulary the proposition which causes all the difficulty – 'the State must worship God' – would disappear. And the realities involved would be much more evident.

[30] Art. cit., *Am. Ecc. Rev.* 124 (May 1951), 331.